Evolving the Spirit Board: Dialogues With Higher Selves

By Luciano da Uno

Disclaimer

With the exception of the author's daughter Gabrielle, for reasons which will become apparent, all of the names in this work have been changed to protect the privacy of those persons, living and no longer among the living. Any similarity to any one known to the reader is a fabrication of the reader's mind or personal reference system, and the author hereby disclaims any such reference.

Dedication

This work is dedicated to the Concept and Being of The One in all of It's manifestations, appearing in this work as our primary contact, WF, as Arch Angels, and as all of those who participated in the sessions, especially the woman who partnered with me to make the initial sessions possible and fruitful beyond my expectations. It is also dedicated to those who are reading it as witnesses who have been directed here by the Larger Hand steering our courses, and participating in what was intended by the writing, and by those Higher Selves who wished it to become so.

Table of Contents

Foreword

What do you want to know, and who do you want to tell you? Do you really have guides and guardian angels? Who or what is the higher self? And is there more than one? Whatever the case, how do you make direct contact?

From where do you get your news? If it's from the mainstream media, you're getting it from five-or-so of the largest corporate media outlets who are all members of the elitists we know as The Powers That Be/Were (TPTB/W or TPTW). If it's from the alternative media, you're getting it from sources who may be as reliable as not, it being a mainstay of TPTW to adulterate those resources with a plethora of misinformation that serves to confuse, at a minimum.

So where do you go to get the kind of information upon which you can most rely? Or where do you go to verify the information that you're receiving from mainstream or alternative media? I'd suggest resort to your Higher Self, if you know how to get there.

This book is about you, in spirit. It is about every aspect of who and what you are to the degree you want to know. It is about the world in which you live, the politics, religions, people, places and things, and about your relationship to them. How do you really feel about something or someone? Why do you feel that way? Have you had past lives? What does that crazy dream you had last night mean? Go ahead, keep asking.

Cut through the glitz, glitter, disinformation, media hype, and programming. Where is the truth in anything? It has been said, of course, that truth is subjective, and that what is true for you may not be true for me. Is that true? Really, there's a conflict you're never going to get past. So what about objective truth? And what does anyone really want to know?

Seriously, if you voted for Obama because you put your faith in his campaign rhetoric, would you want to know that he wasn't even qualified to be president, or that he was CIA mind controlled, responsible for reducing the country to third-world status? Or is Ron Paul really who he seems to be? And why are we really in Libya? Was Gaddafi the ogre he was made out to be? Does any of it really matter? This is where the truth may lead, and if you want to know it, here's a good place to start.

Ouija Board, Spirit Board, Witch Board, Talking Board: proper nouns or not? Is there any difference, or not? Where did they come from, and how long have they been around? How do you use one? This book is not about any of that, so let's dispense with the distractions right at the outset and we can jump into the real purpose of this book: how any version of the board, store-bought or home-made, can be used as an interface with the Higher Self in ways generally unknown and unexplored.

There are many anecdotal reports out there as to the ancient origins of the concept of the board, none of which I've been able to verify. It has been said, for instance, that Pythagoras used a board, and that it aided his investigation of the mathematics that became the hallmark of his reputation as it has come down to us.

I can imagine how he may have hit upon such an idea, but I have personally seen no evidence for it whatsoever. It is certainly a compelling thought, that any one of us could have access to the kinds of tools such a noteworthy historical personage could have exploited for the investigation and development of his life work twenty-five hundred years ago, but I'll have to leave that for speculation.

My intent from the beginning of my investigation into the medium had been to develop my own ideas as to how it might be utilized to obtain deeper levels of understanding about the world we live in, and our own spiritual possibilities as a species and as individuals. This comes primarily as a result of my independent studies in so many areas of human and social development, and the various conflicting theories and ideas as to the nature of reality and spirit.

There is a re-emergence of interest in the talking board phenomenon, likely a result of a combined awareness that something is brewing in the undercurrent of the global society, and on a larger scale, the galaxy and cosmos. There is the 2012 hysteria, ever increasing manipulation of the psychology of terror created, no doubt anymore, by TPTB/W, wars, economic and social decay, all contributing to the level of concern being expressed by more and more people. To have access to a tool that may hold the potential for understanding our place and purpose in a larger sense is an idea that is growing in popularity.

There are a plethora of Youtube videos on the talking board, and Amazon offers a *Psychic Board* complete with a how-to book on its operation. Billed as a *magical message board*, one is encouraged to gather their circle of friends "...for problem-solving, decision-making, creative inspiration, and wisdom." Sounds like an ideal for all the challenges facing the world, and for the individuals in it. My intention was to develop my own methodology for opening the unconscious, or higher self, to conscious scrutiny.

We are beset by distractions and influences that we meet each day without the presence of mind to appreciate the larger meaning and purpose of our places in it. We are manipulated by the energetic emotional intentions of those who have their own selfish motives to maintain a merely physical universe that serves to assure their comfort levels will endure at the expense of the ignorant. Our hope in the larger context of the evolving species of humanity is to inform ourselves of the shenanigans engaged in by those who would enslave us; to know their intent and methodologies; to know our own shortcomings and weaknesses.

For all the books that may be available in the marketplace on the nature and use of the Ouija board/talking board, there is very little dealing directly with the actual potential for accessing the higher levels of being for the purpose of understanding who and what we are in the larger context of the here-and-now. This book is a glimpse of a method to question everything under the sun and beyond, and to make use of the information one obtains to expand human horizons.

As for all that may be available in this first work, it is only a beginning, and we have yet to even scratch the surface. We are exploring, developing and living the New Paradigm that is either flouted or flaunted everywhere without resort to the kind of thinking that will give it life. This *is* that kind of thinking, and it will evolve itself directly from the higher self that understands its potential as a done deal. This is what other books have not explored in any sense whatsoever when it comes to the direct involvement with the kinds of tools that the Spirit Board offers to those who have the maturity and the will to use them.

While TPTB/W manipulate everything to their own purpose by hijacking whatever comes down the pike, this is one medium beyond their reach for those who take the time to develop a skillful approach to questioning external realities, as well as their own inner reactions to events and circumstances. Interactions with anyone and everyone, casual or intimate relationships, are all susceptible to deeper understanding if we can apprise ourselves of more meaningful information about them.

This is not a *how to* book. It is a *what we did and what you can do* book. It begins slowly with a spiritual foundation that may fly in the face of religious tradition - no, it *does* fly in the face of religious tradition. It asks the reader to rise above the fray that holds us imprisoned as separate from each other, each being the jailers of everyone who is not *like us*. It requires the recognition that we are, in essence, spiritual beings projecting into a physical experience.

Yes, I have tried to calculate the slow build to hold the reader's interest while the minutiae of the spiritual idiom are implanted to unlock the doors from the inside. But it is the perspective of the interior universe as it unfolds to create outer realities that has been hijacked, and we are the freedom fighters who will liberate ourselves and all of humanity as we tear down the artificial walls of the psychospiritual prison we inherited from a secret genealogy not our own.

This book is one method of extraction, and I offer it from the deepest reaches of my being, in One. But I don't want to create the impression that I'm a good boy either. We drank a lot of wine for many of these sessions, and the language is frequently as colorful as one might expect in a corner bar. There is no contradiction there: Spirit is everywhere, and being a bad boy doesn't necessarily make for a bad person. The language is as it was spoken. There is no pretense, and I want to dispense with any suggestion that there is.

Human beings operate talking boards as human beings. And even though angels may appear to be heard, they make no judgments. That will be most apparent in the chapter on the visiting Archangels. Human beings dream, and how those dreams can illuminate the deeper recesses of the mind that defy years on a psychiatrists couch is demonstrated in the many examples provided in its own chapter. Do you want to expose the *Shadow Self* that lurks beneath the conscious mind to sabotage your best intentions? Do you think you may have been abducted?

Take this book for what it appears to be: the experiences of real people in real settings who are real sincere, and as deeply spiritual as the deeper reality they've been able to reach. Watch how real we can be, and how deeply we can penetrate into the larger realities, and all the manifestations of the One we can imagine, and then some.

What makes this book different is you, and how you apply the techniques we used to suit your own interest in whatever you consider to be an honest inquiry. If you are looking to summon demons, you don't need this book. But if you find yourself being contacted by deceased loved ones, don't be surprised by the perspective they can provide from their vantage point on the other side.

As for the demons, or the negatively charged discarnate entities, whether they are recently deceased or simply forms of consciousness from other dimensions, watch those youtube videos intended to scare the pants off the viewer. See how casual and careless these immature operators are in giving away their personal energy. Then compare them with how we maintained our deeper spiritual identity in dismissing these same energies, and how quickly they took their leave.

No matter your religious beliefs or your spirituality, you will find this writer embraces the One, and however you identify it, it is always that, and we are each an inseparable part. This book is as deep as you'd care to go into yourself, and into the wonder of creation. It is given in humility and love, in the hopes that it will be used in that spirit.

Whatever this Higher Self is, it is just as surely the guides and guardians who are with us all from a place outside of time, before we even come into time. It is just as surely that superconsciousness to which we are all connected, whether we want to acknowledge it or not. And it is always In Service To Others, and that is you.

Evolving the Spirit Board: An Introduction

We are all guided in some sense or another, by some thing or another. This should be obvious whether applied to ourselves or to anyone we may have taken the time to know at a sufficiently intimate level to see their guidance. Some are guided by fear, and others by love. Perhaps there are degrees of clarity one achieves in being able to recognize where fear gives way to love, or where love is forgotten as fear sneaks in between the cracks.

It is only a matter of what weight we give to guidance, if any at all. It is our own awareness, for as long as we can actually sustain it. I can only suggest that guidance has brought you to this tome, just as surely as I've been guided to offer its substance to the purpose that you may be inspired to your own higher guidance. It can only have been love, or the desire to know love, as the higher vibration intended by the source that inspired this writing, truly.

Certainly I am not alone in feeling that I am here for a purpose; in having felt this way from very early in my life, but hardly able to identify the feeling. It seemed to me that practically everything, every event, had been scripted to bring me to a heightened understanding of our universal purpose as manifestations of the One. Not that I could maintain this awareness at all times, or that I couldn't have been swept up in the events of my life as they were occurring, but more that I could apply very little effort in letting go of the emotional ties and step back to have the larger perspective that leads to the larger understanding.

In the context of purpose, most of us are led on subconscious levels to experiences that may seem on the surface to be negative, sometimes in the extreme. Over time, however, given the pause of perspective, we are likely to see that we could not have arrived at the place of deeper spiritual awareness but for the integration of the soul experience that usually eludes us in the moment of its occurrence.

It has been many years in the making, this path I've followed to this place that defies identification. It cannot be identified except in the hearts of those who have traveled it in spite of their fear, and embraced the courage that is only known in faith. The heart is the faith, and the faith is the courage. The heart, the faith, the courage, all of these are love, and this place where we have arrived is The One. It defies description no less now than it did as we traveled the path that led us here, but we have no need to describe these feelings, only to act upon them as One; as being in the place where the many are One.

What we can hope to attain in continuing to raise our awareness, being in the moment as a matter of course, is a more spontaneous understanding of the inner promptings of purpose as they nudge us along, sometimes in seemingly disparate directions.

It is in the cultivation of faith and trust that we come to the realization that we are being led by forces beyond our conscious, left-brain cognitive facilities, but which nevertheless will rise to the surface of our awareness as we let them integrate with our inner guidance systems to show us the way. We become what we practice, and in this instance, we are honing our awareness to eventually become, at some unexpected point, just that: pure awareness, acting spontaneously in the moment, and merging with the manifestations of the One.

I Am *That*. I *Am*. As I gaze into the eyes of any one, I gaze into my being as One. I *Am* That. When I'm making myself separate from any thing or any person, my Oneness disappears in a cloud of ego identification. If I say that I have been to medical school to pursue the healing arts, and say to you that I Am a doctor, without the awareness that I am only doctoring to heal, in furtherance of Oneness, then I am identifying, and lost to Oneness. I am only one, separate, and there are many.

This is where we see the crux of faction; where divide and conquer assumes its deepest programmed purpose in the outcome that separates us into smaller splintered *ones* that have only their personal enclaves; that need to defend against the onslaughts of those who would threaten that delicate, fragile identity that cannot be supported by the greater identity of Oneness. I Am *That*. I Am. I beseech each aspect of creation to know it, and in that *I Am*.

There is no mystery here. The real mystery is that we would prefer the comfort of programmed beliefs to the eye of knowing otherwise through the sacred organ of the Heart, screaming its courage in defying the control mechanisms of those who have the most to gain from it. They are everywhere apparent in the forefront of every picture we see and every story we hear. But identifying with *their* laws of being makes us them, and in turn makes them invisible.

Identification obscures the true nature of creation, and therefore obscures the true nature of the Creator. The One cannot be identified, and defies identification. The One demands participation *in* the Creation *as* the Creation, and that demands the courage to look beyond identification of the *who* as the *what*. The What is Creation, and the Who is the Creator, the One. *I Am That*. I Am One. I Am separate from nothing, and nothing is separate from me. Our participation without identification is love, where our participation with a programmed identification is fear.

* * *

And so it was in the course of my exploring that I suddenly became aware of a curiosity of inspiration to create what in some circles is known as a Spirit Board, or, in its original conception and design, the Ouija Board. Now I myself make a great distinction in the application of these two different terms, where in the former there is an implied elevated state of spiritual intent, while the latter connotes a mere parlor game. Indeed, the Ouija Board was marketed by Parker Brothers, a manufacturer of popular board games, and has since enjoyed sporadic interest, garnering a host of both very positive and equally negative anecdotal reports, with very spiritual associations on the one hand, and the downright demonic on the other.

To be clear, I take no exception to the Ouija Board in its basic conceptual principles, which, to my personal understanding, overrides the conscious control normally imposed by the left-brain perception of a merely physical reality, and allows the autonomic centers of the body a direct connection to the higher order of right-brain perception.

Jane Roberts' utilization of the Ouija Board, with husband Robert Butts, eventually gave rise to her connection with the now popular Seth entity, and led to her eventual direct psychic trance connection that facilitated a much more responsive interaction with whatever the nature of that source was. Roberts and Butts went on to write and publish many volumes of their sessions, elucidating a plethora of metaphysical and scientific principles that had hitherto no equal in range, scope or accuracy.

The value of the Seth Material, as it became generally known, was for me a next major step in evolving my own understanding of the mystical nature of our truest selves, coming on the heels, and paralleling my study, of Castaneda's don Juan chronicles.

However fictionalized Castaneda's accounts may actually be – and I doubt we will ever know with any certainty, their value to the many who have undertaken the practical study and implementation of those works, among which number I count myself, is inestimable. They have proven to many to have come as a gift from the higher intelligence of Spirit in their potential to elevate our understanding.

In my own reckoning, my own study of these two separate sources, each containing the essence of one higher truth, but set against very different backgrounds, there is the seed of possibilities for the serious seeker to obtain to his or her own personalized integration of body, mind and Spirit.

With all of the foregoing background, and moving on to set the stage for the creation of the personalized Spirit Board that eventually found its way into our lives, it would seem appropriate at this point to introduce Leah, the woman who partnered with me coequally in this endeavor as a function of our many lifetimes doing the work of Spirit.

Our long history was illuminated repeatedly as we progressed through our understanding of the Board's potential as an instrument of information and clarity, where we had to work through our own combined intuition in order to obtain the answers that were not freely given as a function of an unstated requirement of our commitment to involving our own energies.

* * *

When first we met in the early seventies, Leah being around twenty or so, and me two years her senior, there was an instant magnetic attraction that needed no recognition from either of us. Leah had recently completed her associate work at Wesley College, and was still, in my words, possessed of a more strictly construed Christian mindset.

I, on the other hand, having abandoned any notion of entering the Catholic priesthood no later than thirteen years of age, and already deeply involved in the exploration of things much more mystical, had acquired a more liberated understanding of things biblical. Yet we nonetheless found religion to be the common thread that wove us together, and eventually drove us apart.

In the short of it, saving the details for later exposition, after two years or so we parted company on the best of terms, each to go his and her separate ways, until some forty or so years later, when we were once again connected through the same source as our original meeting: my sister. By that time we had each had two marriages behind us, had three children each, and had explored and developed our spiritual maturity to a point that provided a stronger common thread than that which formed the basis of our previous relationship. We were now, it seemed, primed and ready to undertake more serious explorations, marrying our individual understandings as a single mind with the sole purpose of further heightening our awareness of the One. This was an excellent area to investigate as we entered into our study of the potential we thought might reveal itself in the interface of the board.

Board Notes, 2-15-11

Q. Are we soul mates in the highest meaning of the term?
A. Yes

Q. Are we twin flames?
A. Yes

Q. Are we blessed in that sense?
A. Yes

Q. Could we have avoided that?
A. No

Q. Leah's take is that upon our first meeting in this life, she remembered me. Is that right?
A. Yes

Q. So we had alternate purposes that could have manifested?
A. That would not have happened. (quite emphatic)

Q. This was about Leah alone?
A. No

Q. So I didn't have the same recognition of her?
A. No

Q. (L) Did I recognize Luciano?
A. Yes

Q. (L) Did I know it was important?
A. Yes

Q. All of our independent experiences led to our being together?
A. Yes

Q. Even Leah's devastating break up with John?
A. Yes

Q. So we had to have our individual experiences with others as part of it?
A. Yes

In my incessant pursuit of understanding deeper aspects of the relationship we had been developing over the eons I knew we had shared together, I was always finding new ways to elicit new levels of the nature of the reality we were exploring in a heightened spiritual sense.

Board Notes, 2-23-11

Q. OK, I asked this almost the same way when I asked about Leah's role back in Atlantean times, which is that there is no time; we are just a collective of these energies, in whatever space/time we find ourselves. So our being together in that sense is those same energies. We are the same kind of team we were then, as soul mates, but our relationship is more intimate?
A. Yes.

This is not to say that we embarked on the smoothest of paths to arrive at our mutually agreed destination of oneness: there were personal obstacles that remained for each of us to sort through, identify, and vanquish before we could say that we were truly of one mind. After some very serious trials we eventually rallied our combined energies around the concept, design and construction of the Board.

My own knowledge and understanding of others' experiences with such an oracle, if it may be designated as such, allowed us some measure of determining just how we would approach our first session. Yet the immediate results, yielding the appearance of one of my once dearest former friends, some years deceased, created such confusion as to how we would proceed, that we immediately abandoned the session, without so much as a good bye.

Board Notes, 12-14-10

Q. Is this a dead dude?
A. Yes

Q. Is this someone we know?
A. Yes

Q. Who is it?
A. Alan (two letters into it Leah and I both say Alan!)
(session ends)

The next several sessions were not much better, but we had developed a determination that we would push through whatever difficulties we encountered until we were able to make contact with what we could call a reliable source. That didn't happen until some weeks later, when Leah's daughter attended a session, and began asking about her individual guides and guardians.

That became the turning point, as it happened that the entity who eventually emerged from that session was a common guide to all three of us. After some long and protracted sessions, that entity began to develop his own board persona, frequently sending us into side-splitting fits of laughter, and cajoling us into thinking beyond our habitual thought processes in order to create the kind of atmosphere where our responsibility to truth became the predominant motivation for our ongoing pursuit of information.

What we are exploring together in this work is the prospect that we can overcome the program and join in the energy of the heart as one voice that says I Am. As we repeat that mantra in community, we are cementing the larger relationship that is expansiveness. The yin and yang of our existence is the give and take of the principles of expansion and contraction.

I will not pretend that I do not ascribe to the Goddess energy simply because it appears to be unmasculine, nor will I deny the effects of the contractive male principle as it sets upon the thrones of governments in its dominant role as the reckoning force of the universe. The male energy has contracted to itself the resources of the Earth, of the Goddess, and it is from the hands of those few that the power of the individual, as One, must be rescued. I would caution women reclaiming their power as much as I would caution men exploring their repressed feminine energies that balancing those forces is the real key to our liberation. Restoring the Goddess energy is only the first step.

Board Notes, 5-8-11

Q. Is the work that we are going to be doing, the work that we are doing, the energy of our being here, is that more about the Magdalene's energy, the goddess energy?
A. Yes

Q. And is that why I had the opportunity to interact with her [the Magdalene, in meditation]?
A. Yes

We had been watching a television program one night when a commercial for stockings came on, featuring a well known woman singer/actress with killer legs. The ad intended to convey her association with the goddess energy. We had just been discussing the Goddess, and this seemed a synchronicity.

Luciano da Uno

Board Notes, 5-19-11

Q. And [the singer] is not goddess energy!
A. She is goddess distraction

Q. That whole commercializing, you saw what I went through, them commercializing the goddess. When you say she's goddess distraction, you mean that TPTB, at whatever level...
A. They know

Q. So they're using her to distract [from the real goddess energy]!
A. Yes

Q. And this is what I've been getting, and I've been getting this all week, that our purpose is to harness this goddess energy of women into a single directed consciousness, and that's what I want to do!
A. It has its place

Q. So have I been pushing my Magdalene association too hard?
A. You need to understand that we are One.
(V Chuckling)
A. There are no distinctions.

Q. So I have to put my energy more into connecting with... I'm just going to call it the Gestalt. Is that what you're saying there?
A. Yes

I offer this work because the source energy with which we've connected demanded no less than that we work through the conflicting beliefs and dogmatic dictates of the program if we were to ever realize true freedom. Nothing is ever given without the equal commitment of the seeker, and all that can be found at every turn is the One, and it is infinite.

It may seem I am playing with words and phrases here, and I

am, in truth. But this is the plaything of Spirit, creating from the dust of tired programs what may be considered in the light of a new day, if we are only willful enough to recognize that we are ever duped into believing that the same tired thinking that ensnared us will also rescue us. That is insanity.

Our intention, reflected in the invocation statement we honed over time to start our sessions, was to use the board to reach the higher self, in whatever forms it manifested. This proved itself out in the consistent messages of love that became the hallmark of the source energies who became our familiars.

The concept of the One was a theme that permeated our purpose as we explored our lives and relationships in every possible aspect. We were allowed to take nothing for granted in discovering that we were required to work out for ourselves the larger questions we wanted answered. And as we got closer to answering them with our own ingenuity, we were encouraged to conclusions that we could verify.

Initially we asked questions that could be answered with simple yes or no replies, and then evolved the art of questioning to the point that we could receive more lengthy answers. We could make arguments and pose theories, but were never turned away, only directed more inwardly, where we developed clarity. We were cautioned about our own prejudice and bias in places we didn't know it existed, thinking of ourselves as being among the more enlightened, and learning that enlightenment was one of those relative things. We raised our own vibrational levels as a matter of choice, and were given guidance to raise them further.

Our work was inspired by love, and motivated by a desire to discover the programmatic fear instilled over years of living the lie of a contrived social order that hadn't worked in eons. Indeed, we traveled eons back in time to find the roots of the larger social structures that were created to keep us in servitude, and we saw ourselves evolving as through a story we had written from the inside; as having lived it only to write it.

One must also consider this experience in the context of our relationship, Leah's and mine, in our day-to-day discussions of things spiritual, even as they relate to seemingly insignificant occurrences in our mundane lives, as for instance in the work environment. We are always given opportunities to observe the activities and reactions of those around us, and to look for those deeper understandings of how and why others' realities work, or not, for them personally.

To understand the significance of what might appear to be the most mundane occurrences in peoples lives, and tie them to some spiritual principle that opens up a broader array of psychological factors, as one example, and contrast that with one's own observations of a more personal nature as it relates to one's past or present behaviors, is an invaluable developmental tool.

And the fact is, more and more people every day are attuning themselves to higher awareness, and usually without any more guidance than that which comes to them from unexplainable, or synchronistic, sources resulting from their own desires to elevate themselves. In truth, the information we are accessing is as invaluable to the reader as the reader considers it, but it is certainly not outside the realm of the evolving planetary consciousness. If I could sum it up in one excerpt, it would probably be this:

Board Notes, 5-8-11

Q. Is there anything you'd like to impart before we start in?
A. Find your place

Q. Is that in the sense of what the Magdalene said to me?
A. Yes

Q. Well, you know I'm trying. (L) Can I ask, is that place an emotional place?
A. Yes

Long pause, while I try to understand that
Q. Can you give me a sense of what that direction is?
A. Be here now

Evolving The Spirit Board

Q. always
A. Yes

Q. Probably one of the earliest influential books that I had, Baba Ram Dass, and it probably still is in that sense all those years later.
A. Yes

Q. Yeah, OK!
A. Very simple

Q. Thank you. I'll see if I can get that through my over-active mind.
A. Good

It was Leah's suggestion that we had the makings of a book in which we could share the insights we were receiving through the higher self that we considered ourselves as having contacted; the multidimensional aspects about which we can only theorize unless we jump into the possibilities that present themselves.

We were not alone in that idea, because as we proceeded through the sessions we were told that the book had to be written, and that we were being helped and inspired through the source to do it. Who are we to question that in which we had begun to place so much faith, seeing the results expand into something so much more comprehensive than we first imagined?

This is the ever evolving experience we are living as we are able to share it, and it's name is Illusion. Its purpose is to bring us to the understanding of the infinite nature of the One by decoding this ever evolving experience as manifestations of the One, and not merely as things existing in and of themselves. The illusion applies as much to ourselves as to anything else, and we will all eventually come to the place that our eyes are the eyes of the One, looking out and looking in; from itself, to itself.

A Visit From the Archangels

Somehow there had developed a movement from a source whose origins I had yet to discover, that intended to make available to anyone who wished to receive it, a visit in their home from the five most well-known of the Archangels. The idea was apparently spreading with some rapidity through e-mails, and so it was that Leah had received a request from someone with whom she had an ongoing correspondence to become a host for five days.

Now, my traditional Catholic understanding of the Archangels was somewhat programmed to the extent that the Catholic mentality provided for very strict conceptual ideas as to exactly who and what the Archangels were. It necessarily follows that any construction as to their real purpose and intent was also closely controlled by Vatican dogma, along equally strict theological guidelines, so that the Archangels were only what the Church said they were; no more and no less.

Yes, I was just a little reluctant to entertain the notion that the Archangels would actually consent to the idea of being passed-around from household to household as though they were a mere friend, when the Church's view had them in such an elevated status that they might only be approached through prayer or other ritualistic practices. Yet I opened myself to the possibility that we could actually host them as visitors, and listened to Leah's reserved, yet hopeful, description of exactly how the process worked.

Evolving The Spirit Board

When I agreed that it sounded plausible, and the invitation to host them had been accepted, I threw myself into the arrangements with an enthusiasm that actually caught Leah by surprise. We had already gotten to know Gabriel through the events described in The Shadow Self chapter, so based on that familiar spirit, and our interaction having proved to be very casual, I really couldn't justify any reservations, nor did I want to.

Since the accoutrements involved the creation of a makeshift altar, requiring a white candle that would last for five days, a white flower, an apple, and a sealed envelope containing a piece of paper upon which were written three requests, I eagerly set about helping to secure the items. It was my suggestion that we purchase a small potted Gerber Daisy plant from the local supermarket that we knew would last five days, as opposed to a cut flower that might wilt.

After Leah had arranged an altar setting on an end-table, I wrote my three wishes - one for my family, one for the Earth, and one for myself, and placed it under the apple along with hers. We talked about the possibilities for burning the wishes and where we might offer the ashes into a natural watercourse, as was the evolving custom, and then waited the one day we had left with at least some level of anticipation.

I myself admittedly had some minor reservations, but I recognized them as the relics of Catholic programming that could be dispensed with in just as perfunctory a manner as any other dogmatic concepts. I had long ago dismissed such mental clutter in the intervening years since my having seen through the smoke-and-mirrors of Catholicism at around thirteen or so, and this was no real challenge.

The Archangels were to arrive at ten-thirty on the evening of April 4th, and when that time rolled around I had already prepared myself with a centering maneuver I had employed since my late teens. I was ready... or so I thought.

When Leah opened the door, welcoming statement in hand, I had stationed myself about ten feet or so into the room, facing her, and simply opened myself to whatever might ensue. As she began reading the welcome, I immediately felt a rush of what I can only describe as pure energy, and it was love. I offered my own impromptu welcome, and we both relaxed back into our normal state of mind as a couple, occupying our normal abode, no different than we might have been in the company of any visitor.

This was a Monday evening, and Leah had work the next day, so the hour already being a late one, she soon retired to bed. I eventually made myself comfortable on the couch, taking my usual meditation posture, pillow under my butt, one in the small of my back, and settled in to allow myself some level of interaction with what I thought might be an appropriate attitude.

I was hoping for no more than an opportunity to express my gratitude and my wishes for a pleasant time to be shared by all. What I got was a feeling of serenity and release about as normal as I would expect under a typical meditative circumstance, and I must admit that I was relieved that I wasn't engaged in any form of conversation by our guests.

I went to bed not long after, cutting short my usual minimum meditation session to maybe ten minutes or so. I don't remember falling to sleep, or anything that may have transpired in the course of the night; not dreaming, not any movement from Leah, nothing. The next morning Leah recounted the events that had occurred during the night from her perspective, in both the sleep and waking states.

First, she remembered being gently lifted from the bed and placed on the floor, where she proceeded to fly around just above floor level. When she awoke after that thrilling experience, lying next to me, she saw me deep in sleep, yet twitching and shaking in some kind of rhythmic pulsation of such intensity that I should have awakened, but didn't.

The next morning she could only relate the whole affair, and I could but stare wide-eyed over coffee at the thought that I had endured such an event without awakening. Her feeling, and she is certainly qualified to note, was that I had been involved in some kind of healing exercise. Yet at that point there was hardly any thought that we might ever verify what had actually occurred with either of us.

The next day, Tuesday, I took Leah to work as usual in the morning, and decided that my normal meditation time would be dedicated to engaging our guests. Once I had gotten quiet and relaxed, I directed my attention to each of the Archangels individually, silently acknowledging in word what I knew each represented. I mentally held the image of the separate energies in my minds eye before me, saying what came to mind in as humble a fashion as I could muster in a spontaneous outpouring of loving awe.

I was hardly prepared to actually hear the first inklings of responses that would eventually become literal two-way conversations. At first I believed I was merely conversing with myself, it being impossible that one would actually hear the voices of angels as a normal occurrence. But I could not have been more wrong, as over the course of that day I allowed myself the freedom to accept possibilities that had once been the province of children's bible stories.

Tuesday evenings are usually a little rushed earlier, when Leah has her women's meditation group at seven, and afterward, around eight or so, we'll open a bottle of wine, because Leah is off work on Wednesday and Thursday. We set the board up, and casually discussed whatever issues may have been current while we relaxed into the typical TGIF atmosphere of our mid-week weekend.

I had been more-or-less expecting that we would have an appearance by Gabriel on the board, since they were our guests, and he had become somewhat of a regular by then. As happens from time-to-time, I forgot to start the tape after the invocation.

This session also marked the new induction statement, welcoming the most positive spiritual energies appropriate to the immediate circumstances, recognizing the Angels, and inviting them to participate or not as they chose. The first few lines are my recollection of how the session actually kicked-off, which I recounted from a note I made immediately after the first break.

Board Notes, 4-5-11

Q. Hello?
A. hello.

Q. And who do we have with us this evening?
A. Metatron

We are totally stunned.
Q. We are humbled. Is there something you'd like to impart?
A. Thank you for doing this (inviting them to Leah's home)

Q. Of course, we are unfamiliar with you as an Archangel until recently. Is that because your existence has been obscured by the Roman Church and the the powers that be?
A. Yes

Q. Does that have something to do with the fact that you are identified as being responsible for the ascendant energies, our enlightenment, the current path humanity is taking?
A. Yes

I suppose there could be many reasons the Church would have intentionally obscured the existence of one such as Metatron, and in truth, he was totally unknown to both Leah and me until only some few weeks earlier. In fact, in my meditative conversation with our guests, I had singled out Metatron with an apology that he had been totally foreign, my having no knowledge of his existence.

Prior to their coming I had watched some youtube videos describing individual Archangels and their associations with the various areas of human activity, both spiritual and physical, and this was how I had learned of his involvement in our potential for ascension. No wonder the Church would hide his identity when such a leap in consciousness would spell the likely end of the

Church's dominion over the archaic belief system that made it the arbiter of our salvation.

I would have to believe that the majority of the world cultures that actually acknowledge the existence of angels would also conceptualize them as winged masculine entities of glowing energy. I had personally believed that this idea had evolved from the experiential descriptions of those who had enjoyed altered states of consciousness that allowed a direct visual comprehension of the otherwise very ethereal entities. When the tape actually picked up after my realization that it hadn't been turned on, Leah was in the middle of a line of questioning on her favorite topic: orbs.

It may seem to be speculation – or merely projecting on Leah's part, but as it turns out, orbs can actually be, though not always, angels.

Board Notes, continued:

Q. (L) The orb thing with me, was that done intentionally?
A. Yes

Q. And those times when I was playing with the orbs, and they were just so close to me, and I felt that they were doing what I said, and communicating with me, was that true?
A. Yes

Q. (L) Were they Angels?
A. Yes

Q. (L) And they were there just to communicate with me, and to make me fascinated!
A. Yes

Q. (V) So all of the orbs are of a higher density origin?
A. Yes

Q. And when we're seeing them they could be Archangels?

A. Yes

Q. But they could be other forms of higher order!
A. Yes

Q. And they, all of those, are here to assist us in arriving at the place where we're intended to be!
A. Yes

Q. (L)So I just have to keep my camera with me all the time, even though I feel like if I did just snap haphazardly I always will get them; I feel that they're always with me!
A. Yes

Q. (V) So can we assume that when we see them in pictures, the people that they are most condensed around are people whose energy has brought them there?
A. Yes

Q. And Leah's picture of Brewsky (a previous pet dog) with the orbs around, were they there for Leah?
A. Yes

Q. (L) I'm thinking right now of one particular picture of my cousin Susan who is now in the hospital dying of cancer, it was taken two or three Christmases ago after her parents had passed, and in the photograph there is this orb and it is totally encasing her, it is so huge around her. Was that an angel for protection, or was it an angel... (V) What was going on there (in the scene)...
A. She needed protection.

The skeptics among us have commented that there may be some level of manipulation on unconscious levels, and I will not deny that such a possibility exists, and especially where we have seen other personal energies creeping in to muddy the dialogue and the information. Yes, Leah has a very definite fascination for orbs, and yes, this may seem to be the kind of information that is being projected from at least some level of her own psyche in a desire for substantiating a cherished belief. But how do we know anything? Faith.

I can only suggest that we need to be more vigilant in our attention to our own inner promptings, and try to prevent the personal injections we might tend to make into the substance of the information we are receiving in this venue. Diligence is always appropriate to the degree it doesn't interfere with the flow of that information.

And the reader may already be aware of instances where we have had to go through the process of investigating exactly how we may be personally influencing outcomes, as we certainly influence reality in our daily lives, regardless of what we may believe or not believe. It is everywhere evident in the world.

But I digress. I had intended to stay focused on how we were being influenced by these angelic visitors; by what they represent beyond how we may have been traditionally taught to understand their roles as advisers or helpers. I've already mentioned Leah's experience after going to bed, and what Metatron had to say about her recollection just may comport with how the angels are generally thought to be actively participating in our daily lives when we let them. This also demonstrates their great sense of humor.

Board Notes, continued.

(L) I want to talk about my dream. (V) Which one? (L) last night, when I first went to sleep. And I was like zooming around on the floor, like a zooming thing. What was most impressive to me was that I could actually feel the sensation of zooming around on the floor.
Q. (L)Did this company have anything to do with that?
A. Yes

Q. (L)And was it just a matter of like feeling Spirit?
A. Yes

Q. (L)And especially profound was the falling down, which was totally guided, and it was like I was in your arms and I was being placed on the floor.
A. Yes

Q. (L)Same vein of questioning. Luciano sleeping next to me was jerking like he was being electrocuted, but in a very rhythmic pulse for a long time. Does that have anything to do with present company?
A. Yes

Q. (L)And my impression was that he was being healed on some level!
A. Yes

Q. (V) when you arrived last night and I was standing way back off the door, and I felt that awesome energy, was that really what I was feeling?
A. Yes

Q. So when we are open to that, we're actually in a heightened sense of awareness!
A. Yes

Q. Can that be a normal state of awareness for us?
A. Yes

Q. (laughing) And are we gonna look like freaks?
A. If You say so (more raucous laughing)

Then there is my penchant for ruminating, or taking a more philosophical approach to things that I know many people simply take for granted. I began meditating in my mid-teens after I had read Christmas Humphreys' *Concentration and Meditation: A Manual of Mind Development*, which had a profound effect on my cognitive faculties. In later years I pursued every manner of both intellectual and spiritual literature to the degree that I considered myself as being stimulated in more balanced ways than academia could ever offer. So it should not have been surprising I created so much more work for myself in transcribing these sessions when I was compelled to pursue more complicated questions about the very nature of our existence on this plane, and our spiritual origins.

As you will see here, the exchanges that arise between the participants, in this case just Leah and me, can go on at length, and eventually resolve themselves into questions that we hope will be answered in a way that will enlighten and educate. It occasionally becomes rather tedious.

Board Notes, continued.

Q. OK. Well then let me get to this: I have frequently made the analogy that the soul is the hub of a wheel, and the personalities that it manifests to have experience are like the spokes that lead out to the rim of the wheel. Now is that a useful analogy for how the soul operates as far as corporeal personalities?
A. It could be described that way

That's only for my personal understanding. So does that... because I ponder everything, because I want to understand as much as I can possibly understand. And I see that as my nature, so... (L) Because you need to make sense of everything, and that's your way of rationalizing...(V) I think I'm doing that on a more intuitive level, because my further understanding is that the soul that is the hub is always experiencing all of those corporeal personalities at the same time, but we have our focus in one place on that wheel, out there on the rim: we have our individual focus. And in the sense that the soul is the hub (L) but we're all One, you see...(V) Are you talking in the sense of The One, or in the sense of the personalities? (L) We are One. (V) OK, but we are all manifestations of...(L) We are One. (V) OK, the consciousness of the One cannot be expressed...OK, the reason we are here is because the consciousness is infinite, and

the consciousness expresses itself in infinite forms. We are one of the infinite forms, and so we are not separate from it, but we have been given... (L) But why would a different incarnation have a different part of the One? (V) because it gives the One part of its infinite experience.
Q. Am I expressing that in as close to terms as a human could express the One?
A. For you

Q. Is that a useful expression of the concept...and I understand that we cannot really conceive of the One, but is it a useful expression of the concept to help others better understand the nature of their relationship to the One? (waiting for Leah to clear her nose) OK, is that a useful concept for expressing it to others who may not grasp or have a useful explanation themselves for the concept of the One
A. It's not your place to tell them.

So with all of the... I'm just going to call them false religions, proliferating on the Earth today (L) it's all just futile attempts to tell them. (V) No, they are not. They're not trying to tell them anything, they're trying to control them. What I'm saying is... (L) In a way isn't you trying to tell them what a soul is by using the wheel your attempt to control them? (V) No, I don't want to control anybody. I'm looking for a unifying explanation... (L) Well, if it works for you that's good. It's not going to be right or wrong. That's what I'm saying. (V) What I'm saying is... listen to me for a second [because she won't let me finish a sentence]. I'm looking for a unifying explanation that takes the religion out of it, the religious control mechanism.

Q. Now, do I have some deeper spiritual motivation in that direction that causes me to ponder such ideas, or is that just for me, and the rest of the world be damned, and they can follow whatever religious monarch happens to be out there at the time?
A. (unstated, or no answer)

Q. OK, the same evil forces that created the ego are behind all that bullshit... (L) I'm not saying that in a conversation you can't explain how you feel, or how it makes sense to you. I'm not saying that you don't have the freedom to do that... (V) I know you're not saying that. (L) but what I am saying is that you do not have the freedom to say that, my way, what I'm thinking is right... (V) I wasn't asking that. What I was asking was is it a reasonable rational expression, because look, I know as a certainty that this universe is one of infinite universes, and the One as it manifests in this universe is only this universal manifestation of the One; there are infinite universal manifestations of the One for every universe that there is.. (L) and we are, inside, the way our mechanisms work, are an infinite universe. It's the same thing... (V) OK, then let me put this in the perspective of what's going on in the world today. Is the world out of control primarily as a direct result of the tentacles of this negative energy infiltrating our reality and controlling as much as it possibly can, and religion is a primary force in that control?
A. They are obstacles.

Q. So it is not any part of my role (and I'm laughing my ass off here) (L) to enlighten anybody. (V) to attempt to bring some level of spiritual clarity or order to this disorderly world? Just yes or no!
A. Yes, by example.

Perhaps this seems to be argumentative, and we tend to think that it would be disrespectful to assume that we have any perspective worthy of exploring through the use of such devices as argument when we are speaking to the heavenly hosts. But I assure you, these beings absolutely enjoy this kind of banter, or any interaction that recognizes their role in assisting our higher utilization of their energies. This line is one of my personal favorites when it comes down to how they participate on such apparently human levels, which I'll repeat again in context a little later.

Board Notes, continued.

Q. Is that what your energies are intended for on our level?
A. Yes

Q. So you're happy to be doing that kind of thing! (L) I got... (Leah frequently anticipates answers)
A. It's our job (I could only laugh at their use of colloquialisms!)

At this point we had taken a much-needed break, me for a cigarette, Leah for the bathroom, and both for a refill of our wine glasses. This is a usual routine for us when we're into a session that's going as strong as this one. Normally, when we return, we pick right up from where we left off. This was not to be the case tonight.

Board Notes, continued.

Q. OK, we're back. Do we still have Metatron?
A. No

Q. OK, who do we have now?
A. Gabriel

Q. Hello!
A. Hello

Q. Was I facing you today in meditation?
A. Yes

Q. And we had that recognition?
A. Yes

Q. I can only thank you for that!
A. Yes

Q. In a broader sense, your having arrived here was part of a

larger cosmic plan?
A. Yes

Truly, I was happy to find Gabriel waiting for us when we returned, and having seen him that day in meditation, and had that familiar recognition under that circumstance for the first time since our initial acquaintance, I had to ask for his assurance that it had been as I thought.

Although we had first encountered Gabriel on March 15th, when he stepped in to dissolve the negative energies that had manifested that night, and then again when he appeared through the board on March 22nd to explain his previous appearance, Leah took the opportunity to inquire as to his portrayal in a famous painting of The Annunciation by the American painter Henry Tanner. If I can personally say anything positive about the subject, it would only be that Tanner chose to create a standing shaft of luminous form that one might imagine to be the Archangel Gabriel.

More noteworthy is the different takes we each had on Gabriel's identity and purpose, not unlike the separate ideas we'd expressed in his first solo session with us. This one however, had much more religious connotations for Leah, while my more liberated ideology saw it differently.

Board Notes, continued.

(L) And for me, not knowing the larger role of the Archangels, watching youtube today, not knowing that you were the messenger of God, and that you were, in that painting, (V) the Annunciation... (L) that I loved so much, the Tanner painting, that was you in that painting, the messenger of God that harkens the way, that tells someone that something is happening, so for you to come at this time, of the ascension, of all of us ascending, is remarkable to me, and is very profound for me. Thank you very much.

Q. (V) Of course, you know my understanding of the

annunciation, because I've tried to break through the cloud of my conditioning, and I guess this is an appropriate time to ask, I feel some affinity with the Christ character, but not in its historic connotation, and the story we've been given has no relation to the manifestation of the Christ in that era. Is that correct?
A. Yes

Q. But did an Annunciation occur?
A. No

Q. But certainly, in some sense, did you herald the arrival of the Christ Consciousness in that manifestation?
A. Yes

Q. To people kind of like us?
A. Yes

Catholic or Christian, in any sense, you may be shocked by the above statement, and perhaps at some point in the future we can elaborate on the Roman Church's hijacking of the Christ manifestation for their own purposes, namely the creation of an empire that would conquer not just the political state, but the spiritual one as well. Perhaps there are those among you who can relate to the next exchange, since it involves actually taking back our heritage from the theocracy, as well as kleptocratic politicians and the like.

Board Notes, continued.

Q. Was there something you wanted to impart to us?
A. We are glad to be here

Q. We are honored that you are here. Thank You. When I was communicating to each of you today, was that an even exchange?
A. Yes

Q. Because I felt a kinship with each of you with what I understood to be the nature of your....
A. Yes

Q. When Diana Cooper was talking today about Michael I was hit with the idea that he's the throat chakra, but he's also the sword, the warrior, and of course I relate to that, but the throat chakra is the tongue, the mouth, so when Spirit moves me to speak, is that the Spirit represented by Michael?
A. Yes

Q. So can I use those representations of each of you as a guide to what or how those energies can manifest through me?
A. Yes

Q. Is that a part of your higher purpose in those who recognize you?
A. Yes

Q. So there's... I feel like you and I have some other affinity that's tied to my purpose here, and maybe it's the trumpeter. Am I close there?
A. Yes. The battle (that sets me laughing)

To continue, I had intended to illustrate from their own words the particular specialty of each of the archangels in their energetic capacities as aspects of the One, continuing from where we left off. And I'm letting it run to another great example of their incredible humor.

Board Notes, continued.

Q. So you're that guy leading the cavalry and blowing the horn, and Michael is carrying the sword. So of course, I have this other association, and this is what I was saying to Michael today, because I am a warrior, and you're talking about the battle. And I have a lot to learn there, don't I?

A. Yes

Q. And you guys are gonna help!
A. It's about surrender.

Q. Surrender to the higher!
A. Yes

(L) Oh my god. I got something else here. You also have a shield. (V) yeah? (L) That's what I got. You also have a shield. You have a sword, but you also have a shield.
Q. Does one of you represent the shield? (L) Michael has a sword and a shield. (V) Oh, is that it?
A. Yes

Q. OK, Leah really wants to go to bed because she really wants to interact with you on that level. (Leah starts giggling like crazy here, and the disk starts moving) Is there anything you'd like to impart? (the disk is already spelling, and Leah is already calling out letters)
A. See you in your dreams (More raucous laughter)

Who would expect the archangels of religion to have such a capacity for humor; and we're not talking John Travolta playing Michael in a comedy motion picture. This is the real deal, live and in person, however discarnate. Four nights later we were to receive yet another surprise, and yet another indication of the specialty relationships each of the archangels has to some aspect of creation on the Earth.

Board Notes, 4-9-11

Q. Hello?
A. Hello

Q. And who do we have with us this evening?
A. Raphael

Evolving The Spirit Board

Q. Thank you for coming
A. Hello

Q. This is your first appearance here. Is there something you'd like to impart?
A. Yes

Q. Please do.
A. You are loved.

Q. Thank you, We're learning how to understand that. Are we?
A. Yes

Q. You are the healer among the group?
A. Yes

We had been speaking about an eye condition that Leah was manifesting, the specifics of which are irrelevant to this discussion, but Raphael's specific duties in the hierarchy were explored.

Board Notes, continued.

Q. (L)Thank you. (V) Is there something more than just the manifestation of a physical ailment?
A. No

Q. So this isn't something that we should be looking any deeper than what appears to be!
A. No

Q. Wonderful!
A. Make your heart light.

Q. You mean light as in 'the light'!
A. Yes

Q.(L) And also not heavy with worry!
A. Yes

Q. So you work with healers in this realm?
A. Yes

Q. So that means you work with Elise?
A. Yes

Q. And you work with Leah?
A. Yes

Q. (L) And Roseanne?
A. Yes

By way of explanation, the names referenced are people in our immediate circle who are healers, all Reiki practitioners, and with the exception of Leah, practitioners in other fields as well. This was just an affirmation of what we had already understood from other information we had been getting about the various archangels' responsibilities.

I should say at this point, where the narrative has arrived at the fourth day of the visit, that I had begun dialoguing with our guests on an ongoing basis, and seeing them in my daily meditations. We should probably learn to never be surprised by anything that occurs on a mystic level when we are exploring the deeper nature of reality. This is an example that I will allow to run almost its entire course for the value of what was revealed.

Board Notes, continued.

Q. When I was meditating the other night I saw... I believe I saw a woman in your presence. Was I seeing that?
A. Yes

Q. Can you tell me who she was?
A. Mary

Q. The Magdalene?
A. Yes
(L) That doesn't mean anything to me. (V) Mary Magdalene. (L) Yes, I know, but...(V) In her lifetime she was a priestess.

Q. And since I've been pursuing this idea of Jesinavarah, did she have an association with him?
A. Yes

Q. So at least some biblical accounts may be based on actual fact?
A. Yes

Q, So is there a historical record of Jesinavarah as I'm coming to understand his having been born in Lebanon?
A. Yes

Q. Is it known by some to exist in secret?
A. Yes

Q. Is that a secret that is going to be revealed?
A. Yes

Q. And is it in the Vatican library?
A. Yes

Q. So they've known that from the beginning?
A. Yes

(V) I can't wait! (L) Me neither! (we're laughing at that prospect)

Q. But for us the bottom line is that he became Christed and his importance is his having gone through the process to become Christed!
A. Yes

Q. And in some sense, whether we ever achieve it or not, we're

working towards that end!
A. Yes

Q. And as a healer, is that the role you play in contributing your effort to people on that path?
A. Yes

Q. Because it requires a healing in one sense or another!
A. Yes

I frequently see a woman in meditation who has a more amorphous appearance, that is, she has no features that I can identify beyond the fact that she's a woman. I've had this happen now over many years, so I was curious. Again, from Raphael:

Q. I saw a woman today in meditation. Was that also Mary?
A. No

Q. I didn't think so. Was I actually seeing a woman?
A. No

Q. Was... Well, can you explain that phenomenon to me, because it's not that infrequent an occurrence?
A. The energy is feminine.

Q. It's my feminine energy that's producing that?
A. Not you.

Q. So it"s the feminine energy around me?
A. Yes

Q. Leah's energy?
A. No

Q. It's just the feminine energy around me generally!
A. Yes

Q. So was the purpose in my seeing that and asking you to make me more aware of that?
A. We are all both.

Well that is certainly not a foreign concept to me in any sense, and very apropos of the fact that one of Leah's first gestures toward me after recovering from the psychic attack that I describe in the Shadow Self chapter was to give me a book by Lucia Rene entitled *Unplugging the Patriarchy,* which I hope to explore elsewhere.

For the moment though, I will jump forward to another session with WF, where I had the opportunity to inquire further about the Magdalene. But I'll remind those who may not recall, that the Roman Church for years allowed this highest example of the feminine principle to be branded a whore through a mere reference in the bible having nothing at all to do with her.

As a matter of fact, from the perspective of priestly qualifications, the Church is the epitome of patriarchal dominance to the degree where women have always been relegated to the lowest rung of the church hierarchy. Where Mary Magdalene is known in more mystical circles as having been a high priestess in the Christed traditions of ancient societies, the feminine energies would have undermined the corrupted intent of the unbalanced power structures.

What follows had such a profound effect on my psyche that it marked the beginning of the most intimate spiritual relationship that I could ever have imagined, coming at a time when I had fully integrated the feminine ideal in my own life.

Board Notes, 4-10-11, with WF
This occurred the day after the archangels left.

Q. I'm going to move on to the angelic things now. It came out that it was the Magdalene I was seeing in my meditation with the angels the other day, and You're aware of that. I saw her wearing an incredibly colorful rainbow coat, whatever it was. Can you tell me what the significance of that was?

A. Her energy.

Q. Of course it reminded me of the biblical story of Joseph and the coat of many colors. Is there any relationship to that?
A. No

Q. She didn't appear there for no reason, because you people, you energies, Archangels, don't do things for no reason. Can you tell me the reason she was there with them in that circumstance?
A. You needed to see her.

Q. Because I've had some interaction with her in other sojourns?
A. No

Q. So why would I have needed to see her...(L) To balance the boys?
A. Yes

(L) To balance the male/female thing. We see them as male but they're ...(V) they're genderless.

And then, just a little later in the evening, I suddenly remembered an experience form earlier in the day. When I asked about it, and got the answer, I naturally pursued some more background material, and I can only say that we are always amazed at how humor slips in, even without ever using one word to express it.

Board Notes, continued

Q. Did the Magdalene appear to me today in meditation?
A. Yes

Q. And was she telling me to take my place?
A. Yes

Q. At some level do I know what that means?
A. Yes

Q. Is it some place just below my consciousness, that with some work I could understand it?
A. Yes

Q. But taking my place now, that isn't what Leah and I refer to as our mission, or is it?
A. ? (the disk just sat there, no movement, and then all of a sudden, whoosh! – ?)

(I laughed my ass off at that) You are so funny! (To Leah) the way he just waited, and waited, and then... (still laughing)

Some months later Leah and I were having our evening walk on the local track when I just happened to recall her painting *The Colors of Christ*, which involved the head of the Christ in an explosive rendering of colors. I hadn't characterized the Magdalene meditation vision in these terms, but it struck me that her spectral gown wasn't so much a simple representation of the spectrum as it was a resonant embodiment of color. There was some element of the energy that actually resonated with something that was not merely visual, but also conveyed a feeling of the energetic presence.

I mentioned to Leah that I had been disappointed that we were never able to market the painting, which she had reproduced as a *gicleé*, and as note cards. But I pointed out to her that the energetic feeling of her painting was not unlike my vision of the Magdalene, and when we got home I made a note to ask WF about it. I shouldn't have been surprised when I mentioned it in our next session.

Board Notes, 7-13-11

Q. You saw the remark that I made to Leah yesterday about the Colors of Christ and the vision that I saw of the Magdalene with

the Archangels?
A. Yes

Q. Are there similar energies there in what she's portraying in the Colors of Christ and what I saw in the Magdalene?
A. Very much so

Q. Was that the unconscious energy that Leah was tapping when she did the Colors of Christ?
A. Yes

Q. I have always felt that that painting should just take off. Does it have the potential to do that?
A. Yes

Q. So we should be exploring better ways of marketing that?
A. You don't have to. It will present itself.

Q. And is that because the energies that created that painting were source energies?
A. Yes

Q. And even in the sense that you first said to me that I had to understand the source of my creativity?
A. Yes.

The real significance here for me is that Leah had done this painting years before we had even become reacquainted, and when I first saw it I was immediately moved by the idea that it transcended the contrived Catholic myth surrounding the True Christ, and represented what I knew to be the higher energy of the being who achieved the Christed ascension. I know this may be turning some heads, but I hope one day to bring the story of the True Christ to Light, and contribute to the release of those who truly care from the religious bondage of the Church of Rome.

*   *   *

If there is any point I'd like to make about the nature of the Archangels, it is that they seem to be totally devoid of any form of judgment. As I may have said elsewhere, I had been going outside to smoke, and on one occasion I had a substantial amount of wine, but was undeterred in my desire to maintain the communication that had marked the flow of energy between us.

At one point in my rather alcohol influenced state of mind, though nonetheless sober in thought, I started into an apologetic diatribe about my indulging them under the influence, as it were. Not to worry.

Board Notes, continued.

Q. My alcoholic energy last night I'm sure affected my interaction with you, but was that interaction last night as purposeful as it seemed to me?
A. Yes

Q. And was I in fact being told not to beat myself up over that [state]?
A. Yes

Q. So I had the thought that you guys are really here for me to explain it all to myself!
A. Yes

And indeed, my interaction with the Archangels had left me wanting to explain a lot of things to myself, as is my usual custom. But it's their custom not to give answers when a little effort on my part will usually get me to a place where I'll find out I actually know more than I'm aware of.

On a more mundane level, the Archangels not only recognize the nature of our day-to-day lives, they are willing to participate to whatever degree we ask for their indulgence. I had been helping a friend sort through the technicalities of the foreclosure process, and she had a hearing scheduled the week the Archangels were visiting.

I had to ask about the propriety of actually having them accompany us to court, where my friend expected me to sit at her table and keep her focused in the face of certain resistance. My concern was exactly about these expectations and their effect on the outcome of the hearing. This series begins with a question about my own experience in the judicial system some years earlier.

Board Notes, 4-5-11, with Metatron

Q. I guess on other levels I did have expectations that I was gonna get whacked in that circumstance anyhow...!
A. Yes

Q. But that expectation, did that dictate that outcome?
A. Yes

Q. So there could have been a different expectation, especially if I had...
A. Yes

Laughing at the irony of it
Q. So can I apply that same thing to what I'm anticipating Thursday with this hearing?
A. Yes

Q. So I should have expectations for an outcome that I desire!
A. Yes

Q. Well then that brings me to the question: is it appropriate to ask you and the present company of Archangels to accompany us there?
A. Yes

Q. And is it more appropriate to expect that each of you will lend the support peculiar to your individual natures? (L) To Dee? (V) Well, this woman Diane Cooper was saying, for instance, that you can take that orb that's Michael and protect others.
A. Yes

Q. So is that the most appropriate way to... I don't want to say use, I don't want to say incorporate ...(L) Utilize (V) OK, is that the most appropriate utilization of your presence?
A. Yes

Q. Is that what your energies are intended for on our level?
A. Yes

Q. So you're happy to be doing that kind of thing! (L) I got...
A. It's our job
(I could only laugh at their use of colloquialisms!)

I had asked WF about the whole idea of accompanying Dee to court, where I knew I wouldn't be able to say a word, but would have to rely on my ability to keep her focused. We had already had so many discussions about this situation, and this was only days before the hearing.

Board Notes, 4-2-11

Q. I'm not going to ask you for answers here, I'm just going to ask you to help me to try to understand where my energy is moving, because I want to have fun, and whether there's going to be a hearing or not, I have to move on the direction that there's going to be, and I can't talk, but I want it to be productive. So just give me an idea of where my real energy insight is leading me in real terms?
A. Give some space for Source

With all of those factors in place, we went to the hearing, Archangels in tow, though Dee had no idea, and I surrounded her with Michael's light, while leaving space for source. I literally had to hold her down in her chair a few times as the judge tried his best to move her to anger. It didn't work, and she left the hearing with what she wanted, and what I expected.

* * *

Part of the visiting Archangel program is to provide three more people to receive them in the next round of their travels. Elise, Leah's daughter, was having trouble finding a third person, so I recommended my daughter, Gabrielle. There was a lot more to that decision than may be immediately apparent, and I had some reservations of my own about it. Primarily, I had wanted Gabrielle and Elise to become friends, because I felt that they had similar energetic leanings.

Gabrielle had developed a fascination for angels as a child, and she collected everything angelic: statuary, dolls, wall hangings, and who knows what else. She eventually lost interest as she progressed into puberty, but she kept all of those angelic trappings and put them in storage. When I asked her about them she assured me that she still had them all.

Leah and I had been doing a session with Gabriel one evening, when out of nowhere it suddenly hit her that my first-born was named Gabrielle, and she saw some significance, so naturally, we pursued it with Gabriel.

Board Notes, 3-29-11

(L) I just thought of something: why did you name Gabrielle Gabrielle? Your first born was named Gabrielle (V) Because of what it meant (L) And so obviously there's some other things...

Q. (V) and my announcement to Susan that I wanted to get her pregnant was really an announcement of our higher purpose in our union in bringing Gabrielle into the world?
A. Yes

Evolving The Spirit Board

Q. And you know what I was thinking out there when I was smoking about my affinity with Gabrielle?
A. Yes

Q. And is that an affinity with you?
A. Yes

Q. She really is very special, isn't she?
A. Yes

Q. And she depends on me for that more ethereal guidance, doesn't she!
A. Yes

Q. And she knows that, doesn't she!
A. Sometimes

Q. Last night on the phone I was trying to direct her to resort to the guidance the angelic realm could give her. So I really should be encouraging her in that direction? That was her fascination with angels?
A. Yes

Q. Now, does she have an affinity with you that she may not understand?
A. Yes

Q. Can you give me a little bit of guidance in that direction?
A. Her ...(Leah gets 'her namesake')

Q. Is that it, her namesake?
A. Yes

more laughing our asses off (L) there's a reason that you named her that (V) absolutely
Q. And that's her energy!
A. Yes

Q. Is she meant for more than she realizes now?
A. Absolutely

Q. And she really looks to me for that guidance!
A. Yes

Q. So that's what that whole thing was about, wanting to get Susan pregnant!
A. Yes

I beg the reader to consider the entirety of what is included in the foregoing excerpt, because it's all very relevant. Not only was Gabrielle my first child, but she spent the first thirty months of her life in my company. Her mother had a career in the phone company, and after her six month maternity leave there was no question that I give up my trade business and become a stay-at-home dad. Gabrielle blossomed spiritually, being allowed to climb on anything that didn't move away from her grasp, cultivating not only an excellent vocabulary, but an incredible diction that is rare among children. She also became a voracious reader, and still is to this day.

For those who have children, the following excerpt should strike a chord, because we all know how difficult it is to allow our children to thrive on their own, without our interference. Not that Gabrielle needed my interference at all: she was always successful in the things she pursued, and was a responsible young woman in her own right, and became a great mother.

Board Notes, 4-23-11 (with Elise)

Q. She has taken to this idea of having the Archangels!
A. Yes

Q. And I've been guided by them, and probably [by] you too, but I know their energies, and she's accepted that responsibility, and I see my responsibility to help her understand how she can utilize that energy to expand her own consciousness. Is that my

responsibility?
A. No

Q. But I want to do it, so is there any problem with that?
A. Maybe

Q. So I have to tread carefully here?
A. Yes

Q. But I do have the potential to help her utilize the energy of their being with her!
A. She has to recognize the presence herself.

Q. And she has that potential!
A. Yes

Q. So I just have to let go and let that happen?
A. Yes

Q. But I can still have input!
A. Yes. You are her her source.

Q. And that's been our relationship from the beginning!
A. Yes

So while Gabrielle had the Archangels visiting, I asked her to come for a visit with us specifically for the purpose of doing a session, because I knew Gabriel would come through for her while she was here. And he did.

Board Notes, 4-27-11, Leah and Gabrielle at the board

Q. So I just wanted to explore some things, and you know the direction of my energies, especially around Gabrielle...
A. Yes

Q. I would like to explore Gabrielle's background coming into

this sojourn. Is that appropriate?
A. Yes

Q. So can you just give me a brief background of why, for me, why I was so intuitively bent on impregnating her mother to bring her into the world, before we even knew it was going to be her?
A. Did you think you had any choice?

Hard laughing from us
Q. Of course, at that point in my life I was already under the influence of Spirit...
A. Yes

Q. Whatever energy there was between Susan and me, I'm assuming we had some prior agreement to bring Gabrielle into the world. Is that right?
A. No

Q. So was this the spontaneity of Spirit moving the energies and finding the appropriate vehicle to bring her?
A. It was her choice.

Q. Gab's choice?
A. Yes
(G) I win (we laugh)

Q. Can you give me an idea of what that choice was based on?
A. What her soul needed

Q. It was about the energy that she recognized as a potentially incarnating energy!
A. She has a job to do.

This was a mind-blower for me, thinking that I had already had the whole thing figured out ahead of time, and that it was all going to be verified while the Archangels were visiting with her, and she was visiting us with Gabriel in tow. Apparently there was much more to the timing of this whole visitation affair from the beginning. A week before our own visit, Gabriel showed up on the board, and we asked about the upcoming visit.

Board Notes, 3-29-11

Q. (L) Welcome Gabriel (V) what can we do for you? We appreciate your taking the time (although there is no time for you) to be with us. (L) And Gabriel, next week you're coming with your friends (we laugh)
A. Yes

Q. this visitation thing from the Arch Angels, is this legitimate?
A. Yes

Q. So it's not a coincidence that that's happening and we're in touch with you!
A. No

Given what we know about Leah's daughter and our other-life involvement with her as we eventually learned of it, and my own other-life interaction with my daughter Gabrielle; and Leah just suddenly making that connection that night on the board with Gabriel about the names, the visitations seem to have been just as deliberate a chain of intersecting interests as the interwoven affairs between Leah and me over eons. For reasons I didn't quite understand myself, I wanted to get Elise and Gabrielle together somehow, thinking that they would find common interests beneficial to them both. It seems that Gabriel agreed, when we brought the subject up in the same session where Gabrielle's name first surfaced in connection with her Archangel namesake.

Board Notes, 3-29-11

Q. Leah and I were speaking earlier about Elise and Gabrielle

getting connected. Is there a potential there?
A. maybe

Q. OK, is that up to them?
A. Yes

Q. Do they have similar energetic leanings?
A. Yes

Q. And could they in fact become a larger force for good in a relationship?
A. Yes

Q. Now, we can't push that!
A. No

Q. But we can create the circumstances?
A. Yes

discussion about inviting Gab to the Easter dinner, which I nix immediately. Leah keeps insisting to invite them, I tell her my heart says no to the circumstances.

Q. But we have to be more spontaneous in how that happens (Leah keeps talking)
A. Yes

We had Elise for a session one weekend, and out of nowhere I decided to ask WF a series of questions about the possibility of her and Gabrielle forming a bond while she was sitting right there at the board. This also happened to be four days before Gabrielle would be arriving for a session with Gabriel, Archangels in tow.

Board Notes, 4-23-11

Q. Is there some overt reason that you could tell me, that you

could explain to me why I'm wanting to have her involved, especially with Elise?
A. Possibilities

Q. So is there more to it in potential than my wanting ...
A. Yes

Q. (L) does she feel it?
A. Yes

Q. (L) Is that her mask?
A. Yes

Q. So without my actually pushing it, is the energy leading her in that direction?
A. Yes

Q. Is there a potential to be the person to show her that?
A. Maybe

Q. Because it's up to Gabrielle?
A. Yes

At this point I can only say that the Archangel visit was a very positive experience for everyone I know who has hosted them, and that's especially true for Leah and Me, and for Elise and Gabrielle. With respect to my desire to have Elise and Gabrielle get together, they did share the Archangel connection, and for now that's a beginning.

But I can't stress enough how much more we learned by having the access that we did through the board, and that goes for all of us. I think it should be pretty clear from the little I've actually put into this format from those Archangel board sessions that we were able to get so much more, plus the feedback about the ongoing conversations I was having with them that I was able to verify. That just opened another whole realm of experience for me, and I still indulge those conversations when the spirit moves me to do so.

I can only suggest that anyone with a genuine interest who is willing to open their mind to the possibility of actually being able to communicate directly with the Archangels should do so. Have a glass of wine or two, and talk to them, collectively or individually. I was never more sure that I was getting direct responses from them as I was when I would hear answers in my head even before I had finished asking my question or making a statement.

A final note about the visit came after the Archangels had departed, when we ate the apple, which was the only delicious one of the bunch, and then burned the two envelopes of wishes in a baking dish, and transferred them to an envelope. We set out for a spot on the bay, quite removed from the hustle bustle of the local community, down a sparsely populated winding road about a mile long that dead-ended at a high bulkhead overlooking the bay. There were a few houses on pilings in a kind of cul de sac, and some docks where we intended to find a spot with the wind to our backs.

After we scattered the ashes into the water, we turned to see a chocolate Labrador Retriever, dragging his leash, happy as anything, and running right up to us, wagging his tail. We exchanged greetings, if we can call it that, and he went on his merry way, sniffing around, and looking longingly at the water as retrievers are wont to do. As we headed back out in the car we looked at the few houses along the road, all summer residences, to try to determine exactly from where the dog may have come, but there were no signs of life anywhere.

As we were approaching the main road where we would turn, we saw a pickup truck with a cap moving slowly, and tapping brakes. We looked at each other and knew this was someone looking for their dog. The truck made a right turn, and we followed maybe thirty seconds later. He pulled over to let us pass, still moving slowly, so we pulled next to him, opened the window, and asked if he was looking for a chocolate Lab. He was shocked, and appreciative, saying the dog had never taken off.

We told him where to find his dog, and he just thanked us so profusely, still wondering out loud what had gotten into his pet. We went on our way, big smiles for each other, with knowing glances, still high as kites from our visitors. We knew the dog was just following that energy, and naturally, I had to ask at the next board session if we were in fact correct.

Board Notes, 4-15-11

Q. When we released the ashes the other night, and this Labrador showed up, was that ...and then we saw the guy and we both knew he was looking for his dog, and he said he's never run away like that before. Was that dog being attracted to the energies there?
A. Yes

Q. And we both sensed that!
A. Yes

Q. So are we in what you could call an elevated state of awareness relative to where we were before the Archangel visit as a result of their visit?
A. Maybe

Q. So we certainly feel as though we are. Is that the key, to trust the feelings and...
A. Yes

Q. And this is what makes you a good teacher isn't it! (laughing)
A. Yes (laughing harder)

I suggested that a friend just do the ritual herself and not be concerned about having someone actually refer the Archangels to her for a visitation. I asked Gabriel about that, and he assured me they were happy to accommodate anyone who wished to have them visit. There are many internet sites offering instructions which comport with what I understand to be the correct process, and I encourage anyone who wishes to have them visit to just do it.

I've reprinted those directions here as I received them from one of those sites in the word document format exactly as it was posted for those who wish to avail themselves of that inspiring experience.

* * *

The Archangelic 5 Ritual

For an individual the archangels have not been sent to and you want to do this on your own.

Welcoming the Archangels

Thank you for hosting the five Archangels: Michael, Gabriel, Raphael, Uriel and Metatron, and allowing them to serve Humanity, Mother Earth and All Universes.

Choose a date the Archangels will arrive to your home at 10:30 pm. [The actual time is really up to you, but they should depart at the same time as they arrive]

You will welcome and host them for 5 days after having prepared a little altar with:

A white flower

A candle that will stay on the all time they are with you (it needs to be on shortly before they arrive to show them where they are awaited. If needed, it can be blown out when you go out)

An envelope containing a letter with 3 wishes. One for You. One for your Family. One for Mother Earth. Formulate the wishes the simplest way. Not too much detail. Summarize the most you can.

On the envelope, you will put an apple that you will eat only once they have left.

The house must be clean and tidy.

Evolving The Spirit Board

When they arrive in front of your home at 10:30pm sharp, you must open the front door and read (out loud or in your head) this prayer:

“Hello and Welcome to my home, the Archangels Michael, Gabriel, Raphael, Uriel and Metatron. I am very grateful to you for purifying and bringing Peace to this place and to the beings that live in it. I am very grateful to you for bringing Harmony, Joy and Serenity to all of us. I am very grateful to you for granting me my wishes.”

From that moment, the Archangels make things happen.

- It is recommended to meditate and to ask questions during the day. There is no limitation. TRUST.
- They can be in more than one place at a time. When you go out, you can ask them to come with you if appropriate.
- You can sit at a table with a piece of paper and a pen and ask questions around 10:30pm. You will easily get responses this way if your other spiritual channels are not already opened.
- You may be awakened between 3am and 5am with insights and guidance.
- Start to prepare the list of the names and addresses of the 3 people who you will ask the Archangels to visit after you. If you don’t have anyone to send them to bid them well.

When it is time for them to leave:
- Be grateful to them, express all your gratitude. Open your front door and give them the 3 names and addresses where they will be awaited. Wish them a good trip.

Once they have left:
- Burn the envelope with your wishes in order to free the energy to allow them to happen. Take the ashes and drop them in a stream of water (not stagnant water). If you live in a cold country, the kitchen sink is acceptable as the water will be

recycled to Mother Earth. Express your gratitude.

- Eat the apple. It will contain lots of good nutrients and more for you.
- Place the flower outside directly on Mother Earth so that it recycles in a natural way.
- Send this Ritual to the people who will host them next.

Enjoy their presence, you can ask them to go anywhere with you that you wish, during your day.

The Archangels live with you for 5 days, and then rest for 5 days before going on to the next 3 homes. (You can also ask them to return to you for another five days after their rest...this is what many of us have done).

Love, Light, Joy, Peace and Harmony.

The Shadow Self; Meeting Gabriel

"What evil lurks in the hearts of men? Only the Shadow knows"

When it comes to the idea of the multidimensional self, the concept of the Shadow Self is probably older than we can imagine, but at least as old as the idea of evil itself. It connotes a world of darkness and morose feelings.

We have been taught that we live in a dualistic universe, where light and dark are counterparts of an idiom we must accept as surely as day and night, and each is a metaphor of the other.

In this modern era of high technology and sophisticated learning, we are likely to dismiss such notions as the Shadow Self with the explanations provided by modern psychology, according to whichever popularized theory of personality happens to prevail.

Yet as we look around at the decaying state of human existence, we can hardly discount the contribution made by the darker mindset that seems to be dragging us from one justified war to the next.

Are we to deny, for instance, the acceptance of our ability to commit mass murder on a scale hardly imagined by ancestors who had no conception of the possibility of atomic weaponry as a means to accomplish in mere seconds what could only have been realized by the prosecution of wars that may have lasted tens of years?

And that speaks only to the number of lives that may have been lost, without considering the lingering environmental effects of such massively destructive technologies when they are placed at the disposal of those who enforce their will upon the less prepared, with no regard for the larger implications.

It has become somewhat popular in these latter days of the instant paradigm to note the predominance in global politics of what is most easily identified as a psychopathic bent. At one time in history it may have been epitomized by such noteworthy maniacs as Vlad the Impaler, who would plant fields of innocent humans raised on pikes driven through various parts of their bodies.

Certainly this display was intended to discourage resistance to his iron-handed rule, but we cannot overlook the fact that he, and his minions, could only have proceeded through such a course in the absence of any notion of empathic sensibilities.

Yet we can hardly ignore their motivation, where the enjoyment of such heinously perverse persecutions implies something more than the mere assurance of one's continued reign over more pliable subjects. This mentality can only have issued from some darker abode of consciousness totally foreign to the more highly evolved.

We are conditioned in this age of technology to accept the edicts of government wherever the appearances of necessity can be contrived to justify the most barbaric mindset. One need only remember Hiroshima and Nagasaki as examples of the carnage enjoyed by those who have the most to gain in every respect.

Yes, you may immediately spout the reasons for the destruction of these two modern cities, and their non-military inhabitants having to be vaporized, and you will have relied upon the justifications handed to you through the educational vehicle designed to guide your thinking processes without question.

It is exactly at this point that we need to attempt some understanding of how such an acceptance could have been inculcated into the minds of humans when the heart would seem to dictate that such egregious acts are wholly intolerable.

Evolving The Spirit Board

How could the masses of human beings be led to the tacit approval of the wholesale slaughter of fellow humans, when it could just as likely be themselves so set upon when the tables are turned, as they must surely eventually be? It is the Shadow Self, buried in the deepest reaches of the psyche, that condones these atrocities, and worse, in the extreme, actually relishes them.

Blinded by the political propaganda that plays to the emotions of fear, whole populations are frequently swept up in the seeming exigencies that are manufactured for mass consumption by those who would realize the profits in power and money from its proliferation.

People will place logic on hold when sufficient emotional responses are triggered by the instigation of the fear factor levied against an entire population in the creation of an enemy whose origins can be traced to the folklore traditions of demons and dragons. We are so susceptible of these archetypes that we are loathe to question their viability as the perpetrators of our demise.

Now who could have invented such outlandish theories of control, and who would be so cocksure of their impunity as to believe they will escape detection by the victims upon whom the conspiracy is foisted? It is ourselves, in the infinite expanse of consciousness that is our nature. It is the duality we ignore when we are so certain that we have placed our faith in leaders whose own motives must be as purely altruistic as we believe our own to be.

Yet we are duped into an ignorance that presumes our docile nature to the degree that a vast majority will prefer to have the assurance of being protected from the contrived enemy, while a separate element of society will relish the opportunity to express the more vile side of our natures in their participation as executioners, regardless of right or wrong.

The extent of this perverse indulgence is hardly limited to the art of war however, as we are seeing it in epidemic proportions as it manifests in the financial addicts we call the mortgage bankers and Wall Street sharks who become ever more creative in their exploitation of those upon whom they know they can rely for the substance of their greed.

People are put out on the street by these thieves after their manipulation of lawmakers and the economy, destroying the ability of honest individuals to earn a living and pay their mortgages.

The sharks know only too well the nature of their prey, and these unfortunate people will believe they are at fault in their inability to maintain their payments because they have been taught to wallow in a fabricated guilt that lies at the very center of the control apparatus.

Where there may be those less inclined to pursue an understanding of the factors that contribute to our predicament, by ignorance or choice, there are many among us who have labored to inform the more curiously disposed as to how the darker energies emerge. But there they are, even in the broad daylight of our presumably enlightened age, where information would be expected to preclude the possibility of such forces having any chance of prevailing.

Debbie Ford, in her exploration of what she terms the shadow process, exposes the true nature of our totality as human beings. In both film and literary works, she gives us a full-on look at aspects of our personalities that hide in darkness, waiting for the opportunities to reveal themselves in our behaviors without ever a clue as to their commonality as a feature of our being.

In her two books, *The Secret Shadow,* and *The Dark Side of the Light Chasers*, she gives us not only the definitive picture of the Shadow Self, but also the tools to illuminate the depths that are its abode. She provides as well the means to understand the mechanisms of its activities as they surface in the day-to-day routines that we take for granted as we go about our daily lives. And she is not alone in this effort, where even the most ancient traditions have incorporated the knowledge of the Shadow Self in their teachings.

Carlos Castaneda has his don Juan character informing his apprentice that there is a predator who stalks us through the most insidious of means, and that is in the fact that it gave us its mind, in the form of the reptilian brain: fear.

And so it was for us in what seemed an innocent foray into subjects that seemed to be most tame, when exploring ideas wholly unrelated to the Shadow, that it would rear it's ugly head and move in, unseen, until it found the moment to strike. Consider then, the dualistic nature of this particular universe, housing our individual and collective experience, the yin and yang of our being, wholly immersed in a context that we will likely never fully understand while we are preoccupied by the events and emotional responses that are part and parcel of the larger plan.

We were given a glimpse of the darker side one evening while pursuing a seemingly harmless line of questioning, when suddenly Leah remarked that the energy in the disk (our glass version of the planchette) had completely changed, and that the source was someone or something foreign and different. Yes, we had been indulging ourselves in wine, and certainly Leah is more affected by its influence, but that becomes no more than an open window.

Even after we had restored our original source, who I identify only as WF, and questioned him about what had happened, and been satisfied that it had been fully explained, we were surprised on the occasion of another session to have the issue raised again for our better understanding. Yet even that was not the end, as in successive sessions we began exploring it from other angles, only to be confronted full-force by the realization of that darker nature. I am including what needs to be shown to illustrate how this all developed, and where it eventually led.

Board Notes, 3-15-11

This session picks up after we return from a break, :

Q. When you say you tell us we are beautiful, and that its an energy that we have to get into understanding, and that there's some urgency, and that we might be in some imminent danger even, looking around at Japan and... So, are we in some

imminent danger here?
A. No

Q. What this is really about is that the energies are culminating in some definite direction?
A. Yes (big big circular movements of the disk)

Q. And that was a big yes?
A. Yes

Disk starts moving radically, and I tell Leah to take some deep breaths and relax
Q. This energy that's coming into the situation right now is developing a presence!
A. Yes [this is where I should have seen where this could be going]

Q. How have we been doing in assimilating what we've been getting in the last month?
A. its OK
Leah mimics a hippie, wow-type 'it's OK!', and we're laughing our asses off. She says, really, seriously, we're in the zone.

Q. I guess what I'm really asking is if we're on track, if we knew enough to have expectations?
A. You know [this is directed at our ongoing encouragement to have faith, and to trust]

Q. Because we always think there's more that we should be doing, or more that we should know, and we should just make it like POOF, There It is.
A. (The whole time the disk was going, but no response, like it was a moot point)
Leah remarks that she watched it [the disk] going from magic to retarded. Seriously. She goes wild expressing how she was picking up the energy [another sign that went right past me]

Q. Was that an expression of the energy that was going on here?
A. Yes

I explain how Leah was having such a serious interaction, and as she was saying what happened it suddenly dawned on me that she was having that connection. She became scared. We stop. Coming back, I remark that when you're in the moment, everything is irrelevant.
Q. So, are these little moments really momentous in the sense that...you know what I mean!
A. Yes

I have to calm Leah down again as the disk flies out of her hand
Q. She has to calm down her energy, right?
A. Yes

Q. Part of my job is to keep her focused, right?
A. Yes

Q. A left-hand yes, right?
A. Yes.

Q. So we're getting into some kind of energy, so we really have to let go, like big time let go?
A. Yes

[THIS IS WHERE IT GETS REALLY WEIRD]
Q. So all of the stuff we got tonight, from you are beautiful right up to now, like there's some practical...
Leah breaks in to ask me if this is WF, I say yes, but she says it doesn't feel like WF

Q. (L) Is WF here? Who's here?
A. Gab...

Leah says she's getting Gabriel
Q. (L) Is Gabriel here? The Angel Gabriel (V) the Trumpeter?

A. Yes

Q. (L) Gabriel, are you here?
A. Yes

Q.(V) Do you have something to impart? I'm stunned.
A. No.

Q. Doesn't seem that you would want to be appearing here if there wasn't something you wanted. So what's your purpose in being here?
A. Know me.

Q. Does that mean that we should pursue some type of interaction with you here?
A. Yes

Q. Your sudden appearance here is certainly surprising, and WF stepping aside for you, there must be some understanding that we need to have here, given the subject matter. Can you give us a clue?
A. U R beautiful

Q. We are beautiful?
A. Yes

Q. Well, this isn't supposed to be overwhelming, right?
A. Yes

Q. So this is meant to reinforce the whole direction of the energy that we have to get with to understand what's really going on here, the bigger picture?
Leah remarks she's getting weird. That it was awful, and weird. I agree.

Q. We'd like to have WF back please, and a hello would be OK.
A. Hello

Q. WF?
A. Yes

Q. What was THAT about?
A. I M Sorry

Q. Was that a negative energy?
A. Yes

Q. And where was that slipping in from?
A. Leah's lost place [I really should have seen this coming from the developing dialogue]

Q. We should say goodnight?
A. No

Leah says she doesn't feel as young as she did before, and that thing that happened, that was not a part of her. That was her lost place. I ask if she feels like she was being invaded, and she expresses that she felt like she wasn't even supposed to go there. Like 'somebody rescue me'.
We Pause. She explains that the weirdness was that she was confined, or blocked. I felt like someone was trying to lead us, or trap us.
Q. So I suppose we had our lessons tonight, didn't we?
A. Yes

Q. Is there anything you'd like to give us before we leave?
A. When will you know that you are loved?

Q. I can only say that that is a parting thought. The essence of what we were being given tonight.
A. Yes

Q. Thank you WF (L) I can't help but say I feel a little nauseous. It was that profound, right?
A. Yes

Q. Good Night.
A. Good bye.

The next night we attempted some kind of explanation that might make sense on a level where we could understand something that strange, outside the context of our normal experience. But I was also starting to understand that '*when will you know that you are loved*' was all about understanding that we would be protected. And we were. I had pondered that idea after the session, into the wee hours of the morning as I made continuous trips out to the garden to smoke, indulging the starry sky, and the hugeness of what we were into. We took up the issue of the dark energy again the next day.

Board Notes, 3-16-11

Q. Hello?
A. Hello

Q. And who do we have with us today?
A. W...

Q. Is this WF?
A. Yes

Q. So, what a night that was! Any comment before we get started?
A. Did you have fun?

We laugh our asses off
Q. I guess in the confusion you could say we were having some fun, did you?
A. No

Q. (L) Sorry. (V)Obviously that was all very very heavy, and there was a larger purpose to it that we have not yet comprehended?

A. Yes

Q. Is that something that was all meant to sink in as time goes by?
A. Yes.

Q. The Gabriel entity that snuck in, was that in fact who we know to be the Arch Angel Gabriel?
A. Yes

Q. But you said it was negative. I asked was that a negative energy.
A. (ccw) Yes

Q. Normally, Gabriel is not associated with negative energy. Can you tell us why it was negative?
A. Dark energy

Q. Is Gabriel normally associated with dark energy?
A. No

Q. So is this the yin and yang of his identity?
A. Yes (and Leah was getting the other side, the duality)

Q. So why did he jump in with that 'you are beautiful' just as you did? OK, was that cynical?
A. No

Q. So then why as a dark energy was he jumping in with that?
A. He recognized you

Q. So we should derive a positive message from that negative experience?
A. Yes

Q. (L) It was kind of like exploring your shadows, the shadow side?

A. Yes

Q. You reminded us that we are not of this world. Is that in the sense that Jesus proclaimed I am not of this world?
A. Yes

Q. (L) Is that all of humanity that is not of this world?
A. No

Q. (L) Because we are all one. (V) Is that because so much of humanity is mired in the physical world, that they can't conceive of not being of this world?
A. Yes

Q. And our energy should not be distracted by that?
A. No

Q. Can we move on?
A. Yes

While it may not seem relevant, I included the few lines about not being of this world, even though we are in it, simply because I believe the trap to which we are all susceptible is exactly that idea: that just because we are in it, we are also of it. Christians among you will recognize this as a primary idiom of he who is called by history Jesus. It hadn't yet hit me that Gabriel's recognition of us was the recognition of the dark energy, but not his.

Again, while we thought we had been given the explanation of the events with the dark energies, we were eventually set-up to receive yet more information about it. But this was not to be given freely, and here you will see how hard one has to work to get down to the real meat, and still not get what is asked for. A week later we were surprised by an appearance on the board that we were never expecting.

Board Notes 3-22-11

Q. Hello?
A. Hello

Q. And who do we have this evening?
A. Gabriel

Q. Gabriel, hello!
A. Hello

Q. And what can we do for you, or what can you do for us?
A. I was trying to protect you.

Q. You were trying to protect us!
A. Yes

Q. From what or from whom?
A. Dark energy

Q. OK, you were trying to protect us from dark energy?
A. Yes

Q. Was WF aware of that?
A. Yes

Q. Is that what he was trying to communicate to us afterward?
A. Yes

Q. Where we were seeing what we can only consider to be (L-Bad feelings) the yin and yang of identities, that was not your energy?
A. Right

Leah comments there's no RIGHT on the board, and she was looking for it.
Q. So are you free to tell us what the source of that dark energy was?
A. No

Q. Are you free to tell us what the intent of that dark energy was?
A. You might not understand.

Q. You know what a junkie I am for knowledge, information, whatever it is, you must know that!
A. Yes

Q. So in that context would I want to know anyhow?
A. ?

Q. Well, what, do you think that knowing that might be so threatening to me that it might evade my understanding?
A. ?

Q. Are we getting into territory where you would be violating my free will in my knowing that?
A. ?

Q. Is it a matter of my free will?
A. No

Q. (L) Is it a matter of his well-being?
A. (No audible answer)

Q. You know. Is this something I can handle, or not?
A. Not

We laugh our asses off
Q. We were making identifications with archangel origins: is that you?
A. Yes

Discussion. Leah says that he's about nurturing, about loving and understanding. (To me) Is that your understanding of Gabriel? (V) Not at that level, no. My understanding of Gabriel is as a mouthpiece. (L) Gabriel is a mouthpiece? (V) Yes, the

Trumpeter. He's the Trumpeter. He heralds the Word of God.
Q. (L) Is that what you do?
A. Yes

Q. But, what she's picking up, your being loving and nurturing, is that also you?
A. Yes

Q. So why would you have intervened in... (L) You would think that somebody like Michael would have intervened...(V) No, what I'm saying is what's the significance...I just had the realization that you are probably in infinite places at One infinite time. Is that right?
A. Yes

Q. So your expansiveness has you here, there, and everywhere in the instant that is not!
A. Yes

Q. But certainly your attention is directed... I guess in the nurturing sense...is that where your attention is directed here with us?
A. No

Q. So where is your attention directed here with us?
A. You are beautiful

Q. OK, we are beautiful. OK, so let me ask this, and I used the word the other night talking to WF, is this, just for lack of a really... because this is amorphous enough for both of us, is this a gestalt, in the 'you are beautiful' gestalt, and you are beautiful is everywhere, now?
A. You are not of this world

I had walked outside earlier to smoke, and as soon as I looked at the night sky (as I always do) I was overcome with the pragmatic knowledge that I am not of this world, and even stuck my head

in the door to tell Leah.
Q. And you must be aware of that realization I had stepping outside the door tonight?
A. Yes

Q. Now, are you, or other energies around us and you, feeding this in some way?
A. Yes

Q. And the feeding is the gestalt!
A. Yes

Q. So I was saying earlier (when I came in from smoking and the realization), in the place where we are not of this world, is where you are always with us, because we're always there!
A. Yes

Q. And so it's just dawning on me that it's really time to dig into that not being of this world as much as we already know we're not?
A. Yes

Q. In fact, Leah said earlier that when somebody says we are not of this world, we are in it, she goes Duh!
A. Yes

Q. And this energy is on the planet now!
A. Yes

Q. In fact, the planet is this energy!
A. Yes

Q. So, we're just tied in with all these other people, all these other levels. At the level where I am, those people are here!
A. Like minds

Right! Which is what I've always asked for.

Evolving The Spirit Board

Q. At some point we're going to be actively, outwardly involved with like minds in the consciousness raising!
A. You are already

Q. (L) We're looking for something really profound and it's just....Oh, it's going to spell something else because it just came to my head
A. Just be

So Generally, let's take Leah and I one at a time...generally, how would you say I'm doing at my just being in spite of the fact that I can't just be? (looking at Leah) Yeah, how am I doing at ... cuz (L) You can just be, because that's all you ever are. (V) OK, but I have my...(gets into a long discussion about the observer, and just being is when the observer is out of the way. It turns into one of those tape-wasting distractions that goes on forever.) Then I make the observation that Ascendance is Transcendence.
Q. Is that pretty close to how it is: Ascendance is Transcendence?
A. Yes

Q. And that's our work, to transcend?
A. Yes

Once again I've let the dialogue run to points that may not seem immediately germane to the subject matter, but I think it equally important to see how these sessions evolve, and how we are allowed to explore larger issues to understand exactly how involved the work becomes. Note that no matter how hard I push to be told what I want to know, we are continually denied, and as it turns out, when the realization comes to Leah in another session with WF, we are finally allowed to discover the true nature of what those dark energies really were, and how the duality is always there, waiting to surprise us at a moment where we let down our guard. But we had attempted to explore this area with Gabriel only two nights prior, and should have seen already, once again, where it was leading.

Board Notes, 3-29-11, with Gabriel:

Q. When Leah and I had our alienation last year...and it's about a year now. And I felt that she was under a psychic attack, was she under psychic attack at that time?
A. Yes (immediate, strong reaction, so much so that Leah says WHOA!)

Q. And was the intent of that psychic attack to keep us separated?
A. Yes

Q. Is this those dark energies?
A. Yes

Q. And when they were trying to interfere and you intervened, was that their purpose?
A. Yes

Q. So, were either or both of us doing something to attract that dark energy?
A. No. Just beliefs

Q. Those dark energies are intent on interfering with us?
A. Yes

Q. And we're not alone in that?
A. No

Q. So metaphorically, this is the battle of light and dark!
A. Yes

Q. In fact!
A. Yes

Q. (L) So when I start to feel, like, it doesn't feel dark, it felt familiar. The dark forces that took me over were familiar, felt...yeah, no, I was rejecting everything that I knew (V) related to me (L) yeah, and the truth (V) your heart (L) and saying no (V) OK, and so they were familiar (L) yes, because what I wanted was familiar; it was the same road that I always...(V) and was that familiar in the sense that that's her program?
A. Yes

Q. (L)So that's what they meant by beliefs (V) yes, so they used the program to get in!
A. Yes

Q. (L)And that's how they always get to me (V) Well, that's how they always get to everybody, but when they use the program on me, it's about guilt isn't it?
A. Yes

Q. And that's why you keep reminding us that we are loved!
A. Yes

Q. OK, and that we are beautiful!
A. Yes

And pages later, that very same evening, as we are traversing the list of questions I usually have at the ready, I have a further insight that causes me to return once again to the subject of the dark energies, this time as relates to what I have referred to as the psychic attack upon Leah. The advantage of the board work is that you can keep returning to the same issues from a different direction until something clicks, that is, if you really want to get to the bottom of the kinds of personal issues that ultimately lead one to understanding, and to freedom .

Board Notes, 3-29-11:

Q. Now, more ethereally, the dark energies were trying to come through the board that night, and you stepped in and intervened!
A. Yes

Q. And those are the same dark energies that were behind the psychic attack on Leah!
A. Yes. Only stronger.

Q. Did you, and/or your realm, and/or the positive energies intervene in bringing Scot to give Leah that message? [Scot is a psychic medium, and had provided information to Leah in a group setting that caused her to look towards other men for a solution, until she realized that I was actually the other man]
A. Yes

Q. So, in that sense, is that evidence... I don't like to use that word, of the protection we have working for us (L)demonstration of the protection (V) yes, demonstration?
A. Yes

Q. So while we may have to be careful, we can have confidence that we'll always be protected!
A. Yes

Q. And you were saying that the psychic attack on Leah was even stronger than what happened on the board that night!
A. Yes

Q. And while she was being psychically attacked and I knew that, was I being guided to maintain my cool and not...
A. Always

Q. So I can always rely on the higher guidance when I take my ego out of it!
A. Yes

Evolving The Spirit Board

I explain to Leah my desire to keep feeding her the important little things in e-mails while she was under attack, and she admits always getting out of bed in the morning and running down to see if I e-mailed her.

Board Notes, 3-31-11 (with WF), the final understanding:

Q. The dark energies that tried to interfere on the board, and the dark energies that were responsible for Leah's psychic attack, are they the predatory energies that came out in the Castaneda don Juan books?
A. maybe [once again, nothing given freely; we have to work for it]

Q. Are they generally predatory energies trying to come through the board that night, and Leah's psychic attack?
A. They are personal

Q. And in the sense that they're personal...they're not our personal energies!
A. Yes [meaning, they are our personal energies]

Q. Oh! (L) Is that like [the] shadow [self]!
A. Yes

Q. (L) So, at times, when they become strong, is that triggered by some kind of outside manipulation?
A. Yes

Q. (L) It's basically fear, correct?
A. Yes

Board Notes, 4-2-11 (with WF), picking up the theme one final time, and the answers to the question I had been asking from the beginning:

Q. The shadow, and what happened that brought Gabriel in to

intervene that night, he basically just said that 'you don't want to know, and I'm not going to tell you', and you're aware of that!
A. Yes

Q. But when we talked to you the other night, you intimated, and I think Leah actually said 'the Shadow', that it was - and I'm realizing that words have meanings and you guys know how to work the words, (both laughing) - you guys know how to work the words, right?
A. Yes

Q. But, Leah specifically asked if what was involved there was our shadow energy, and you said yes. Now forget how much we really understand about it, that's a line of questioning that we can pursue?
A. Yes

Q. The shadow energy side of ourselves we can't really know in a positive life time, is that right? (L) What do you mean a positive lifetime? (V) We can't ... because we can have negative lifetimes. We have negative lifetimes in the shadow self. Do we have negative lives in the shadow self?
A. Yes

Q. And that's why we just have no conception about what that kind of life is about. Is that right?
(L) Oh God!
A. Yes

Q. And that was the energy that was coming through that night?
A. Yes
(L) that's incomprehensible! (V) That's right, incomprehensible, and that's why... (L) I knew that was from us (V) right, you got that sense.

So there it was. In a moment of clarity, when we were innocently pursuing another line of questioning, we got the answer to the question that Gabriel knew we were not ready to hear. The dark energies were our own, or, as I believe from studying the transcripts, seeing how Leah on the occasion of the dark energies suddenly taking control of her 'channel' on the board that night, was predisposing herself to leaving an opening for them to slip through and attempt to dominate.

And while we were thinking that they were the darker side of Gabriel, a seventh density, higher vibration not susceptible to such an attack, it was originating from Leah, and all the signs were there in my attempts to calm her down and focus her just before they manifested; Leah's Lost Self, as WF told us immediately after he returned. Gabriel had merely stepped in to rescue her before it got out of control. We are loved, and so we are protected, once we accept the awesome power involved in letting go to the One.

And I think this may be an appropriate opportunity to explain our invocation on every occasion before we open a session. We initially began with this: *We invoke the energies of the combined higher Self as a point of contact*. I had originally composed this induction in the belief that our combined Higher Self would wield sufficient power of intent to allow only the highest vibrational energies to manifest on the board, and that would afford us the protection we required for such an undertaking as we were intending.

On the second day that Leah's daughter joined us, we had occasion to receive a lesson of critical import from WF, where we were led to believe we had a recently deceased woman appear on the board, who in spite of our best intentions to help her find the light, led us into a blind alley. At the point we were throwing up our hands in frustration, WF stepped into to tell us it had been him all along, and that we had failed to adequately protect ourselves by invoking the power of love.

Thereafter, I wrote an addition to the opening invocation: *We invoke the energies of the combined higher self as a point of contact, in Love, with open hearts and open minds*. I can hardly begin to imagine how those dark energies may have succeeded in whatever the darker intent of that personality aspect may have been, had we not previously invoked the loving energy as WF suggested on that occasion. Invoking love, we are always protected by love.

This proved to be quite adequate, until we had the occasion to host the Five Archangels; just another synchronicity in what was quickly becoming a continuous line of same. That opened another chapter in our ongoing effort to open ourselves to Spirit with the highest intention of making ourselves a tool of the One in the evolvement of the spiritual collective that is everywhere manifesting on the Earth plane, for those who are so inclined to the work.

We hope we have seen the last of the dark energies in our own lives, while we are also quite certain that they are doing well in the world at large. This is everywhere evident in the many psychopaths and sociopaths at the highest levels of governments around the world, promoting wars, genocide, sanctions that starve innocent children, and worse.

It is only in the personal heightening of awareness, meditating upon the highest good, raising the global vibration, that we will bring the darkness under the scrutiny of the Light. We who are dedicated to the mission of the consciousness raising that is occurring are a growing number, ensuring that fewer places are available for the Shadow, who knows what evil lurks in the hearts of men.

What Are You Talking About, Other Lives?

Now here is a subject around which some considerable controversy has arisen. Among New Agers (a term that I have no fondness for), it is certainly more acceptable to believe that our multidimensionality allows for far more in the way of our deeper and more complex natures as human beings. Reincarnation is only a relatively small portion of the expansiveness that many of us include in that conceptual awareness which we are only beginning to understand.

Religious sentiment provides a potentially dangerous argument when biblical citations are brought to bear in the mix of what may or may not be true. But what might be called truth in the experience of one, may be a verifiable falsity in the theoretical domain of God's Word. So here is the crux of the issue where the rubber meets the road: what is the experience of the primary protagonists from each side of the argumentative aisle?

On the one side we have the accepted dogma of the collective religious traditions who represent the fear-based perspective of heaven and hell. It is not unlikely that some number in this category have experienced heightened sense perceptions that they dismiss through the rational dicta of left-brain logical ideologies.

The other side offers the freedom of exploring different possibilities that more likely than not offer only momentary transcendent explanations with the promise of personalized interaction through a source beyond logic. Individuals in this paradigm have escaped the strictures of pure mathematical formulas for living, recognizing that the deeper sense-based perceptions incorporated into the human mechanism have a higher purpose beyond rational understanding.

My goal here is to present these glaring opposites not as unresolvable polarities, but as the tension and release of the energetic ebb and flow that is the One, as we are of it. It is probably already apparent that my own experience is of the more esoteric variety, flushed in energetic similes of unknown dimensions that are meant for exploration. It is not the province of my logical processes to ascertain false values through contrived theorems of right and wrong: they have no place here. Where religious viewpoints dominate the conditioned perceptual apparatus insofar as they obscure and preclude transcendent awareness, no purpose in being can ever be served.

I am in the company of innumerable millions who have the kinds of experiences that so defy explanation they take on an aspect of the unknown one can only associate with the Source. And so no explanation need be proffered where experience lies within the realm of creation itself, which we know with certitude that we will never comprehend. One must be a part to have the highest comprehension possible.

When I was originally daydreaming about the questions I would like to pose to a higher frequency self beyond my normal conscious access, I contemplated experiences that I learned through faith in my higher sense perception were as real as walking down a street. What is real, anyway? I knew the experiences I wanted to explore through the medium of the board would blossom into a contextual environment that would lend itself to my contribution as a force of creation. And it has.

I have energetically sought and found other co-creators exhibiting the same sense response to their experience as I, and coming each to their personal place of comprehension as diverse parts in a whole that are the whole and the parts simultaneously, in the instant of the quicker perception that embraces the infinite moment. To be in that moment is not to be in the program, and to have the speed of perception to be aware when even the moment can become a program. I was guided to conceive of the board as a tool beyond what I knew had yet been done to satisfy my own personal evolutionary process. And I am doing just that.

* * *

It is difficult to pinpoint when I began having personal spontaneous glimpses of other lives lived, as I'm sure many can appreciate. Those glimpses are all wrapped up in the daily encumbrance of learning the program, where younger minds are being taught to identify the trappings of fantasy as it interferes with the inarguable sanctity of logical reality.

Over the years I've learned to spot instances where others may be relating an early memory that I immediately see as an other life recall. Leah was relating the story of a doll she had gotten so early in her life that she didn't remember never having it. She called the doll Edwina, saying she had always been fascinated by the name. As soon as I heard the story I informed her that she had been, or been around, Edwina in another life. But she also said that she became equally fascinated by the name Cynthia from the time she first heard John Lennon's song for his first wife.

I had to ask about that, not just in the sense that I knew Edwina was another lifetime, but also in the sense that I knew Cynthia was a programmed response; a product of the culture that had little girls swooning over the icons that were the Beatles, and everything having to do with them, from wives to mothers.

Board Notes, 5-19-11

Q. Something else just to get out of the way: Edwina and Cynthia. I don't know so much about the Cynthia thing, but when she (Leah) told me the story about the name Edwina, and I immediately said 'that young, that's another lifetime'. Is that

another lifetime for her, Edwina?
A. Yes

Q. (L) Was it a baby?
A. Yes

Q. (V) Her?
A. No

Q. (L) Was it my little girl?
A. Yes

Q. (L) The one that that psychic told me she saw me twirling her in the air, that one?
A. Yes

Q. (L) And I don't have her here now!
A. Right

Q. (L) Will I have her here in this lifetime? (V) You mean be around her! (L) Will I be around her in this lifetime?
A. Yes

Q. (L) Will she be a baby?
A. Yes

Q. And that's good karma isn't it ? (Leah is crying as I ask)
A. Yes
(to Leah) Don't cry honey, because this just reinforces how much of your life is supposed to be tied up in babies.

Q. Is that right?
A. Yes

(L, still crying) But she won't be my baby. (V) Yes she will. They'll all be your babies!
Q. (V) All babies will be Leah's babies, right?

A. Yes
See, that's where you have to be honey!

Q. Is there some kind of connection like that with Cynthia also?
A. No

Q. Just John Lennon's wife!
A. Yes

This is not just a simple factual reportage of a simple event. This is an emotional rendering of a relationship that crosses dimensional boundaries with such force and power that it actually rekindles the mother/daughter bond to the extent that Leah is instantly transported. Pure fantasy is what the logical left-brain makes of all this, but then again the left brain has been completely cut-out of the process. What would any doctor of psychology say about that? I don't know for sure, but I'd guess it would involve a lot of behavioral science and Freudian analysis to discover that poor Leah is suffering some kind of delusional repercussions because her mother deprived her of the nurturing that she then projected into the little girl self that was her innocent doll, Edwina.

Phew! I've got to wrap my head around that. How easy it is to get past all that complex contrived science when we can have more surety in what we know is a valid experience that we can be left to contemplate on our own, and find the validity from the more dependable barometer of the heart.

* * *

Other lives, for those who may actually ponder them in the context of the larger mystery, are more often thought of as a sequential line of experiences that add, one to the other, to a totality of cumulative understanding. I cannot be alone in my own more expansive imaginings when I think of the unfathomable mystery that is the human condition. We struggle to make sense where there can never be any real rational understanding of such phenomena.

I would have to guess that my own understanding has grown out of the plethora of works I've managed to read over the years, from Edgar Cayce, the twentieth century's most noted introduction to the subject, to the enigmatic Seth of Jane Roberts. It was the Seth Material in all its volumes that led me to ponder the impossible dilemma of complexity that presents itself as the universe we think we know when we study modern scientific explanations of the nature of reality. And Stephen Hawking assures us that there is no god in his mathematical calculations.

So who am I to challenge him, when my relatively tinier mind shudders incredulously at the sheer mathematics of Hawking's complex universe? Surely he perceives some higher order that escapes me to the point of my insignificance as a figment of the creation's mathematical imagination. Yet I am unable to leave the subject alone, absent the inclusion of mathematical certainties beyond my present intellectual capacity.

I put my ideas to Metatron one night during our visit from the archangels in an effort to make some justifiable universally acceptable conclusions that I might then proffer to the equally curious, wherever they are. This inquiry eventually became so protracted that I abandoned it for a much-needed break because I found myself being challenged by Leah when the larger concept of The One was added to the mix. I've recounted this particular exchange elsewhere, in the Archangels chapter, comparing the soul to the hub of a wheel, and readers may refresh their memories as they choose.

But I got exactly what I was looking for, and whereas I had never broached this subject before in a session, I had wanted to take it much further. Of course, I was operating on the assumption that all consciousness springs from The One, and I had no desire to explore that idea, simply because it was already a basic assumption giving rise to the creation of humans as an expression of The One. So I suppose that what happened after that statement is what could only be expected in trying to discuss something of such complexity with anyone else.

I had introduced this subject months before, prior to our taping the sessions, so I was transcribing from copious notes that I had to take with my free hand, as one was usually on the disk.

Board Notes, 2-8-11

I described my own understanding of non-sequential lifetimes, which would explain my life now as compared to my life as Apollonius.
Q. Does that come close to explaining non-sequential lifetimes?
A. The time is not relevant

Q, That means it's an open-ended, open-middled system?
A. Yes (This seems to confirm my version of the explanation)

In an even earlier session, I first raised the issue of the experience that seemed to have verified a life as the first century sage, Apollonius of Tyana, which I will return to shortly. But there had been one of those surprise sessions where we found ourselves dealing with a discarnate entity, which I cover in more depth later on. Upon reviewing that occurrence in a later session, the idea of sequential time versus non-sequential time came up.

Board Notes,

Q. So, just as in the case of Mozart, where his energy has already projected back into the corporeal world, other...OK...Our other personalities continue with their identities even as newer personalities become corporeal. Is that pretty much how it is?
A. Yes

Q. because I'm thinking of my having woken up as Apollonius. Apollonius is still there, and the aspect that is Luciano just merged with him for that experience.

A. Yes

So therein lies the premise for the existence of all that could manifest as consciousness, and more so in the nature of human beings with innumerable lifetimes of incarnate experience as infinite expressions of the One. My intention here had not been to take the subject any further than the investigation into the very real phenomenon that we call reincarnation, but the problems that arose in attempting to explore it, even with someone who knows me well enough to appreciate my more inquisitive approach, highlights the more complex nature of the subject as it might be broached with a more general audience.

But there is one more complexity that I doubt will ever be resolved, and that lies in the fact that several authors have reported these forays into other-life existences where they displace the personality into which they have projected. The most famous of these is probably Robert Monroe, the father of sophisticated brainwave entrainment technology, and the author of several books on astral projection.

In *Journeys Out of the Body,* Monroe relates several instances of finding himself in a dimension where he repeatedly projected into the body of an individual over several years, completely displacing his personality. More recently, Felix Wolf reported a similar experience he had one time in his *Art of Navigation.* Obviously, since my Apollonius experience was so similar, I had to put it to the board, and see just what I could discover about the deeper aspects of such a phenomena.

Board Notes, 6-2-11

This guy Felix in The Art of Navigation talked about that experience that he had jumping in to someone else, and Robert Monroe also talked about jumping in to someone else. And of course, I had the Apollonius experience. Now, are those examples that I just gave all examples of the same general nature?
A. Yes

Q. So I was jumping into an other-life personality jumping in to Apollonius!
A. Yes

Q. Did my consciousness displace the consciousness of Apollonius in that moment?
A. Yes

Q. Was Apollonius aware of that?
A. No

Q. So none of these personalities... so is there missing time for them when that happens?
A. Maybe

Q. Well, in the case of Apollonius, he was an enlightened individual. Is that correct?
A. We see him as being.

Q. An enlightened individual!
A. Yes

Q. What I'm trying to get to is... (L) How could that happen? (V) Yeah, how could that happen, or was there something larger going on....
A. Yes. Always

Q. and this is not just simply a matter of what I'll call bleed-through!
A. Right

Q. So, that was happening for me!
A. Yes

Q. So was it being triggered or at least to some extent involved with Tim's crazy accident that day that he also had a similar experience in my Apollonius experience? Were they tied up

together?
A. Yes

(L) Did he have an accident? (V) Yeah, he was having an accident while I was having that experience. Remember I told you? (L) So it was psychic. (V) But I didn't know he was having an accident. (L) That's what I'm saying. It was psychic

Q. What Tim was doing having an accident at that moment, did that have anything to do with triggering that experience for me?
A. No

(L) You were remote viewing, through Apollonius. Because you didn't believe you could do it. Only an enlightened being could do it.

Q. The circumstances that I viewed in that Apollonius experience, did they really occur. Tim jumped in the water and hit his head?
A. Maybe

Q. OK. Was he in that lifetime with me as Apollonius?
A. No (long long time answering that)

Q. I was transposing characters in what I was seeing?
A. No

Q. Did the event that I witnessed actually take place whether it was him or not?
A. Maybe

Q. Is this something beyond my understanding?
A. Yes (these answers were all coming with surprising immediacy)

Q. OK. So when I first... my first conscious recollection of

hearing the name Apollonius of Tyana was when I was reading the Borderland Journal, and it just set the alarm bells off. And that was my first inclination that I and that character were one!
A. For that minute.

Q. Right. OK. In consciousness!
A. Yes

This went on a little further, but this is just another example of how other lives are entangled with our focus personality in ways we are probably incapable of understanding. Jane Roberts alluded to this mystery in several of her books, where each of the personality's activities influence all the others through time.

* * *

Other lives likely reveal themselves in more common activities that we tend to take for granted as the normal processes of the mind, such as daydreaming and sleeping dreams. If we are not disposed to considering that these activities may carry the potential for larger states of human experience then we will simply dismiss them for the tired normal explanations that make life easier to comprehend.

I have had many other-life revelations in the waking state of daydreams where I knew as a certainty that I was viewing other aspects of my more expansive self. I have also had a few regression hypnosis sessions that manifest that same daydream quality, and I know many people dismiss such guided sessions as being their own fantasy imaginings. My experience says otherwise.

The single most appropriate example of spontaneous other-life recollection was one of my earliest and most vivid adult daydreaming experiences. Coming from a Catholic family, I had an aunt on my mother's side, Aunt Joan, who was a nun. For some seemingly unknown reason, she and I were always butting heads, and somehow religious issues always surfaced even where the conflict may have had nothing at all to do with religion.

On this occasion – and I don't remember the particular circumstances, I found myself viewing a scene where I was a Catholic monk in the American Southwest, probably Spanish. I had a close laymen friend who, though not outwardly religious, was nonetheless sufficiently possessed of religious superstition to believe that I would suffer the eternal damnation of hell when I announced to him that I was leaving the priesthood. This friend possessed all of the physical attributes of Aunt Joan, with the exception that he was obviously male. He was tall like her, had all of the facial characteristics of her, and although he was not in any sense religious, had that same superstitious nature that is frequently apparent in the demeanor of so many nuns, in my experience growing up around and being taught by them.

A curious aspect of such daydreaming visions is that the visual phenomenon is accompanied by another dimension of internal knowing that informs the mind of the particulars that are in no way actually communicated through what one is viewing. So I knew without a doubt that this was Aunt Joan, and I knew that her commitment to the convent in her present life was a direct consequence of her having taken such a position at my announcement.

But there is another part of this story, and that is my having come under the influence of the indigenous people of the Southwest, where my religious beliefs had completely collapsed under the weight of what I had experienced in exploring their spiritual culture, and the mind-altering effects of entheogenic plants.

Moreover, in my present lifetime I had been disposed to entering the priesthood from early childhood, but had been saved by scholastic distractions, and finally introduced to the same psychedelic liberation as had been responsible for the previous monastic rejection. I explored this example on several occasions at the board, and was astounded to realize that the primary personality who was the source in our board communications had also been the protagonist in my Southwestern transformation.

Evolving The Spirit Board

I explored these particular experiences over several separate sessions in a somewhat scattered series of questions where other lives had come up in any number of ways, and I learned more about them each time.

Board Notes, 2-16-11

Q. I had snippets of a lifetime with Aunt Joan, Sister Mary Anne, in the Southwest. We were both men, and I was what seemed like a monk. Was that accurate?
A. Yes.

Q. And did I come into contact with local natives where my belief system was radically altered?
A. Yes.

And regarding my previous relationship with this source:

Board Notes, 3-2-11

Q. Have we known each other in corporeal existence?
A. Yes.

Q. Were you responsible for my awakening in the Southwest?
A. Yes.

And then, in yet another session:

Board Notes, 4-2-11

Q. What I call my bad trip. Was that something that had...was that something in the nature of intervention because unpredictable things had happened in my life, and in don Juan's terms, my world had to be stopped?
A. No

Q. Not that I'm making a case for psychedelics, but there is a

case for psychedelics, isn't there?
A. If you say so.

Q. Well, OK. Look, when you and I knew each other in the Southwest experience that you verified for me, was there psychedelics involved in that?
A. Yes.

Board Notes, 5-8-11

Q. Is that something you would have taught me when you were my teacher?
A. Yes

Q. And I have the power to remember that!
A. Yes

Q. And really, that's why I fell right into the don Juan thing, because I was falling right back into being your apprentice again!
A. Yes

And here, I had always been feeling some kind of severity from WF, and frequently joked about it. Eventually I realized that I was reliving the feelings I had being under the watchful expecting eye of a teacher, and naturally I had to ask about it.

Board Notes, 4-10-11

Q. Did you hear the remark I just made to Leah about you being the severe teacher?
A. Yes

Q. Could you relate to what I was saying there
A. Maybe (causing much laughter yet again)

Q. But it is that way sometimes in the sense that you are more-

or-less putting your foot down!
A. Yes

Q. And I know you are incapable of taking offense! (laughing)
A. Yes

Of course, in the previous instance I had no idea of where this was going to lead. But one of the repeated themes of the sessions was learning to understand our feelings, and to follow them to the conclusions where they led. Occasionally I would think of certain things I wanted to question this source on, and I would get these feelings, and then one day it hit me.

Board Notes, 4-15-11

Q. I would like to start here, because we went into this thing the other night, and I'm sure you're well aware of this. You and I went into this thing about the strict teacher. Now this is about understanding feelings, because we're learning to understand what our feelings mean. So that feeling that I was expressing, and the way I feel sometimes about you, I'm seeing that as just a rekindling of the relationship we had, the feelings I was familiar with when you were my teacher. Is that what this is?
A. Yes

I knew that.

Q. and does that have the effect of helping me to understand my feelings better?
A. Yes

Q. Wonderful. You are a great teacher!
A. Yes (more laughing, as usual)

More recently, when I realized the math had me incarnating more frequently, with very short temporal time periods in between lifetimes, and I had the sudden realization that WF and

I had been with each other many more times than I'd initially thought, of course I asked about it, and got the answer before I finished asking.

Q. And I was just talking about the experiences I've had being so close together. You and I have worked together many more times than just that...
A. Yes

So here is a perfect example of the inner promptings of what may seem merely idle curiosities, but they contain the kernel of something that spans the temporal limitations of our existence in this particular dimension we call linear time. The more attention we pay to these promptings, the more familiar they become, and we find ourselves opening pathways to a higher understanding. I found such an example when a close friend was visiting

* * *

I hadn't seen my friend John for some years, though we had always stayed in touch through e-mails and telephone. I hadn't said anything to him about the board sessions, but I very carefully broached the subject when he came to visit. In the very early years of the internet we had chosen screen names. Unbeknownst to him I had been intending to use the name Merlin, and much to my surprise, he announced that he had chosen the name, with the suffix of his birth month and year. I fell back on my second choice, Cicero, suffixed with my day of birth.

When John excitedly announced that he wanted to do a board session, we covered some number of subjects that were of mutual interest to us both. At a point where it seemed appropriate, I asked about other life relationships I had suspected for some time that we shared. I know John was completely blown away, because this was not a concept he had ever felt compelled to investigate.

Evolving The Spirit Board

Board Notes, 5-10-11

Q. John in this lifetime is my closest intellectual confidant. I don't know how else to say that, which of course is a need of mine. But we also have a familiarity which lends itself to thinking that we have had other experiences together. Is that the case?
A. Yes

Q. And I'm honing in on the Cicero time, is that...
A. Yes

Q. And that was apparent in both his and my interest in Cicero, is that right?
A. Yes

Q. So now, you know the story behind Merlin's screen name. (To JP) You don't know the story behind it...
A. Yes

Q. And how, and my association with Merlin...
A. Yes

Q. Does John also have an association with Merlin?
A. Yes

Q. So does this go back even much further than that?
A. Yes

Q. Even as far back as the Atlantean times?
A. Yes

Q. And he knows a lot more about that than he realizes?
A. He knows way too much

And I have to continue on with this observation I made in the notes as I was transcribing this, first because WF just finds these incredible opportunities to insert his humor, and second because he is using a phrase I get somewhat often with respect to how my own curiosity has led me over the years, much like John's.

Board Notes, continued:

Leah and I were already laughing at the point he used the word 'way', because we know how WF makes his little points with humor. We quip back and forth with JP. I compare my own affair with Gabriel telling me the same thing. Then WF breaks in:
A. You can understand that he needs to know like you.

(V) Wow! That he needs to know like you.

Q. Is that what we're doing here tonight?
A. Yes

Q. Because he has a much bigger role going on here than he realizes?
A. Yes

Q. And is he expressing that energy now in what he's trying to do politically?
A. No. It's a distraction.

That gets another round of serious laughter. (JP) That's what we were talking about. (to Leah) We were talking about that earlier.

* * *

Another curiosity that seems to transcend the dimensional constraints of temporal reality is the peculiar occurrence where we may be involved in some kind of activity prior to a session, and find that it has bled over energetically across the temporal barrier to merge with personalities from other life experiences, long since deceased, but apparently still connected to us at some level. Leah is well aware of my feelings about Mozart, or Volfie as I like to call him. There certainly is no question that Mozart is one of the most profoundly prolific and gifted composers in history, but I always thought that his music was predictable in the sense that from my earliest acquaintance with his work, I seemed to know exactly how and where it would progress.

It was a Wednesday evening, our weekend, since Wednesday and Thursday are Leah's days off. We had opened a bottle of wine, and Leah was on youtube indulging some of her favorite music. I had been going in and out smoking in the garden, and engaging the Archangel Gabriel, with whom I had developed an ongoing special relationship, ruminating and conversing on those magical starry nights that are so frequent. On my trips back into the house I was engaging Leah's musical interludes, singing and dancing. We started a session much later than we ever had, shortly after eleven o:clock at night. When we finally got on the board and through the invocation, Leah had already picked up a new energy.

Board Notes, 3-30-11, 11:00 p.m.

Q. Hello?
A. hello

Leah remarks "If this is true, you're not going to believe who we have tonight. I don't even think you like him"
Q. And who do we have with us tonight?
A. Mozart
(L)Laughing. It's Mozart. It's him. It's him. I got him before he even spelled out his name. He's here. Seriously, he's here.

Q. OK. Go ahead. It's your board. How are you finding your way here?
A. You have no idea!

(L) He's crazy
Q. Do you know of my association with you?
A. Yes

I have to get Leah focused, because he's taking control in her mood.
Q. You know from the earliest that I listened to your music I could always anticipate every next move!
A. Yes

Q. And why is that?
A. You don't know how to count.

We are just busting up laughing
Q. Of course you understand that we'll be analyzing all this after the fact, but for this moment, what has brought you here?
A. You

Q. For what purpose?
A. To tell you that you are beautiful

Q. This is because of my affinity with you? Our Affinity with you?
A. Yes

Q. So this is the 'you are beautiful gestalt' pulling Mozart out of the 18th century to reinforce this energy!
A. Yes

Q. Because we just have to give up and jump into the ocean of this energy and go with it?
A. Yes

Q. (L) And it really does have a lot to do with music, doesn't it?
A. Yes

Q. And Leah was into that whole music thing tonight, is that it?

A. Yes

Now this is a long excerpt, but there are two points to be made here. First, Mozart was picking up on Leah's musical reverie across the temporal boundaries, and we hadn't yet even explored the nature of the connection that was responsible for that. Second, we had no prior board connection to Mozart, nor were we aware of any other connection to his persona. Apparently his reference to my not knowing how to count stemmed from some involvement I or we had in the eighteenth and/or nineteenth century with the character we know historically as Mozart. This was one I couldn't leave alone.

Board Notes, continued:

Q. So let's get back on track, because we are so much more than we think, do you mean we are so much more than we think in our multidimensionality?
A. No

Q. Do you mean we are so much more than we think in terms of our role here?
A. You are going to knock your socks off!

Laughing our asses off. (L) Where the hell did that come from!

Q. So you're just, right there, you're just indulging the nomenclature of the times!
A. I guess so!
More laughing

Q. Do we have some association together in other experience?
A. Yes

Q. Are you around now, not as Mozart, but...
A. Yes

Q. (L) Do we know you?
A. No

Q. (L) Will we meet you, because I would like to. Will we meet you?
A. Yes

(L) We will! Oh, I can't wait (very excited at this point)

Q. OK, we are going to knock our socks off in terms of what we're going to accomplish in our mission?
A. Yes

Then a little further on, after exploring a few other items that came up in the course of this unexpected conversation:

Discussion about Mozart's music and my feelings about it while I get more wine.

Q. The remark about my not knowing how to count, you can probably see from where you are the way I count music, and how much into rhythm and meter I am...
A. Yes

Q. ...so is that an inside joke between you and me? (L) Absolutely
A. Yes

Q. From other times!
A. Yes

Leah gets into her seeing Mozart and me in other times being musicians [composers?], arguing about it, and him accusing me of not knowing how to count.

Q. So, is there anything else you want to relate...and believe me, we appreciate what you've related so far. (L) Are you

anything like that guy that played you in Amadeus, because when I think of you, I think of that guy in Amadeus, and ...(V) Did he accurately represent you?
A. Yes

Q. (L) and that whole, like crazy thing that you did, I loved that. If I was like alive in your time...He's going to say you were (disk was already moving to respond)
A. You were

Q. (L) And were we together?
A. Maybe

So there it was directly from Mozart's own mouth, from his perspective not as one living in his time, but apparently outside of it, acutely aware that he was already incarnate in our time, and that we would eventually meet up with him. He also verified our relationship with respect to his remark about my not knowing how to count, a musical reference, intimating a more professional kind of closeness, and that we, or at least whoever asked the question, were around in his time.

Does this satisfy any of the other-life parameters I have been trying to establish in this chapter, or is it all just so much wishful thinking? Certainly it could be considered as being very subjective, but then it must be a subjectivity Leah and I are sharing, as it is our combined energies at the board.

After Mozart's departure we continued on with the session, which is our standard course of action when we are initially greeted by a discarnate entity. We were surprised to find Gabriel waiting for us, and my immediate questions to him were about the exchange we had just had.

Board Notes, continued:

Q. So obviously, you were aware of that little exchange between us and Volfie!
A. Yes

Q. Do those things happen spontaneously?
A. Yes

Q. And that was because of Leah's musical thing tonight!
A. Yes

The next night we took up the subject of Mozart's visit with our regular source, WF, for more insight, and we got it.

Board Notes, 3-31-11

Q. I'm really curious about the Mozart thing, because I asked if I was a composer in another lifetime, because I felt I was. And you did your 'maybe' or '?' thing, and then I said I just prefer to think I was. Now, is that a past relationship I've had with Mozart?
A. Yes

Q. And Leah's musical indulgence last night was likely the energy that brought him here!
A. Yes

Q. But it was our joint familiarity with him in other experiences that opened up that energy?
A. Yes

Leah remarks about knowing him in this lifetime, and I remind her he said we would.

Q. (L)Will we get to meet this person?
A. Yes

Q. Because he's a like mind obviously!
A. Yes

Q. (L) He seems like he's a crazy whacky person. Is he?
A. Yes

Q. Obviously his coming through the way he did had more of a spiritual intent. So there are entities with whom we've had relationships that are now, some aspect of them is now on that side, and they're just joining in this gestalt that is expressing itself now, and through us, inclusively!
A. Yes

So now we discover that the visit from Volfie was not merely to say hello to old friends, about which relationship we were now more certain, but to join us in our present purpose as positive forces in the evolving consciousness that is making itself evident everywhere on the planet. This was Mozart's reference to our being beautiful, and knocking our socks off in terms of the mission we are presently involved in. But I think there's just a little more, and that is the suggestion that we will be meeting him in his newer sojourn in our present time. And I must say, I've already identified him, and he is a she, and well known in the goddess circles.

Moving on to other spontaneous experiences I've had that were grounded in other lifetimes, I can point to circumstances in which we find ourselves manifesting abilities that have no possible origin in the present life. This is similar to Leah's Edwina doll, where a previous life experience carried over into this one, but my actual manifestation was in a highly evolved skill, and I had explained it away with a rationalization that I had learned it from a television show.

* * *

I regularly visited a girlfriend in State College, Pennsylvania whose closest girlfriend lived in a house she rented with her boyfriend. On one occasion when we were visiting, the girls had run off somewhere, and the boyfriend and I were left in the living room, where there was a large working fireplace, above which were hanging a set of fencing swords. I remarked that I had always loved the idea of fencing since the television series

Zorro had first aired in my childhood. The boyfriend was on the fencing team.

He suggested that we have some fun, and that he would give me some basic instruction. He took down the swords and handed me one. Before he could say a word I had already swished the sword, pointed toward the floor as you see them do in the movies, to get a feel for its heft, I suppose. He immediately remarked that I had done this before, and I assured him I had never held a sword until that day. As he raised his sword and I took the position I had seen Zorro take so many times, en garde, he remarked again that I must have had some experience, and that I had been putting him on, so to speak.

I again assured him that I had never touched a sword before in my life, except that maybe I had played Zorro as a child with sticks or some such. Well, after we had our first parry and I bested him almost immediately, he became quite angry, saying that I was playing him, and I again reassured him that was not the case. We parried twice more, and twice more I bested him directly to the heart, and he refused to go any further. That event always stood out in my memory.

Board Notes, 3-29-11, with Gabriel

Q. My swordsmanship with that guy at Penn State, State College, is the Spirit of the warrior manifesting in this lifetime to do this work?
A. Yes

Q. And there is real swordsmanship experience in other lifetimes!
A. Yes

Q. But I'm given these little peeks at those other experiences to reaffirm my warrior position now in this critical time, and especially in what Leah and I are doing!
A. Do you doubt?

(I laugh my ass off)

Q. Or do I affirm?
A. maybe (LOL)

Then, in another session, we weren't really talking about any specific subject matter; just jumping around. Out of nowhere I asked about a look I had adopted and maintained for a couple of years. My always long, curly, and now substantially graying hair was complemented by a mustache that could have been a handle bar if I had groomed it that way, but I didn't. It simply extended well beyond the ends of my mouth in a rather frayed style, and was highlighted by a slender goatee that began just below the lip, and left my chin almost completely clean. I called it the Musketeer look, and it was exactly that.

Board Notes, 5-3-11

Q. My musketeer look, and it was a musketeer look: was that a throwback to another time?
A. Yes

Q. Is that the swordsman's lifetime?
A. Yes

Q. Was it anybody of note?
A. No

Q. But was it in the warrior spirit?
A. Yes

Q. And was it a lifetime that I worked in the positive energies?
A. No

Q. Ohhh, I was a bad guy!
A. No

Q. OK, but I wasn't directing my energy in positive ways!
A. Right (more raucous laughing)

So there was another example of another lifetime sneaking in to surprise me, where I had absolutely no idea what was actually manifesting at the time, and believed quite innocently that I was learning something of a very complex nature in a very high art form merely from watching a television program, manifesting the appropriate musketeer appearance only many years later.

But I have to suggest that such things go on all the time for many people. In fact, I remember Edgar Cayce saying that certain people who were incarnating in the twentieth century from Atlantis were capable of resurrecting the skills they had misused in that lifetime and using them for good in this one. How many may have actually done so I cannot say, but I can imagine it is as equally frequent as it is unrecognized.

* * *

Having covered the manifestations of other lives as they reveal themselves in dreaming, daydreaming and unrecognized actions in the normal course of our daily lives, we are left with what is likely the most well-known area of other-life recall: regression therapy, or hypnotic regression. Since I have undergone a few of these kinds of sessions, I can readily identify the single most common problem with this methodology as being the disbelief of the subject in what is being recalled, or viewed.

Evolving The Spirit Board

There are generally two levels of hypnotic trance, and varying degrees of each. Practically everyone has experienced what is known as the hypnogogic state, a condition manifesting either just before falling to sleep, or immediately upon waking. This state is characterized by visions, sometimes of vivid dream recall, by what are known as out-of-body experiences of varying degrees, or even by hearing voices. I believe there are no limitations to what one may actually encounter in such a state.

Guided hypnosis can generally take the form of a light, relaxed state of awareness at one end of the spectrum, or what is known as the somnambulistic state, where one is so deep in trance that there is no awareness, and usually no recall at all. Dolores Cannon has written many books based on information she receives from her hypnosis subjects in these very deep somnambulistic states. She is able to move these people to all manner of times and places, seemingly without limit, and elicit experiential memories of an absolutely staggering and unusual nature.

My own experience with regression hypnosis came when I offered myself as a surrogate subject for a former girlfriend who suffered many years from chronic digestive track disorders. While I had never heard of acting in a surrogate capacity in hypnosis, I theorized that it was likely very possible because I had actually acted as a surrogate for this woman before we ever met.

I had been studying with a group of healers in Florida, and was living in a relationship with one of the women who was a very gifted healer. She had been studying a very complex system of muscle testing that isolated the various bodily organs and metabolic processes, and I had been her guinea pig many times as she practiced the trigger points. When she expressed her desire to diagnose her friend some twenty-five hundred miles away, and I knew from my own experience with my children and the chiropractor who was treating them that surrogate testing worked, I volunteered to sit for her.

There was no doubt as to the efficacy of the substitution, as my own familiar reactions to the process were nowhere evident as I was tested in surrogate for this woman who I had never met. But when we did finally begin talking over the phone, I suggested that she undergo regression hypnosis, as I recognized that her digestive problems likely originated in other lifetimes. We eventually met in person, and engaged in a relationship over several years, but she could never bring herself to attempt any form of regression.

After we parted company, but still remained intimate friends, I continued to suggest hypnotic regression, and when she finally relented, I found someone in my area who was a reputable and qualified hypnotherapist, and arranged a session for myself just to see how it would work out for me personally before I undertook to attempt a surrogate session. The result was surprising.

That first session yielded two separate life experiences, the second of which took me completely by surprise. The therapist eased me from the conclusion of the first reliving, took me to a very tranquil setting, and told me look at the first scene that presented itself to my view. I thought I was in ancient Rome, since I could see that I was wearing what looked like the garb of a centurion. I looked at the walls of the city from the outside, where I stood, and realized with a start that I was in an even more ancient city, and the terror of the people instantly told me I was in Atlantis.

I suppose the immediate reaction of the reader might be that everyone claims to have had a life in Atlantis, but it seems that may be more fact than fantasy. As Edgar Cayce and others have said repeatedly, many of us are here to work out the karma that we accumulated in that period, when many people fell into the trap of the myriad distractions and indulgences that proliferated there. I won't speak to my own likely indulgences, because this series of events didn't seem to include any.

When I told the therapist that I was in Atlantis, she asked me to describe the scene. There were violent earthquakes and storms, and the people were panic-stricken, running in every direction. She moved me to another scene and asked me what I was seeing. I was in some low-lying mountains that I could see gradually rose to some higher peaks, and white, seemingly stone buildings were interspersed along the gently rising slopes. At the top were some buildings that I knew were some kind of scientific installations.

A picture arose in my mind's eye that some kind of electromagnetic probe had been drilled to a very deep level into the Earth inside one of these buildings, and somehow it was connected to the atmosphere. I was thinking that it was the ionosphere, and I knew that what these scientists were doing was so dangerous it had created many of the devastating events I was witnessing.

I had the distinct awareness that I was a high-ranking officer in the military, and that I was responsible for transporting a wise old man from the continent, though his countenance escaped me. In the next scene I was evacuating a party of people from the buildings I described earlier, when suddenly there was a collapse, and I was trapped in the rubble. I advised the party to leave without me, and to be sure they provided for the safe escape of the wise man. Although they initially refused to leave me, I ordered them to do so. My back was broken, and there was no hope that I'd recover.

Suddenly I was being beamed aboard a disk-shaped craft, and the beings, who I could not make out, tended to my broken back, and I found myself on a ship, at sea, with the original party whose safety was my responsibility, along with the wise man. I could never conjure an image of this man, but I knew that his wisdom was of primary importance in establishing a new culture on the remnants of the one just destroyed. Eventually I saw that we had all made it to a large cave structure in Central America.

Naturally, when I had the opportunity to investigate the more salient facts of this adventure at the board, I did so. And again, I did this in small snippets as I was jumping around from one thing to another, over several sessions, and over many months as things would be triggered in my daily life.

Board Notes, 2-16-11, noon

Q. Some things I wanted to get to last night. The first is that series of regressions I did for Shali, and this Atlantean experience came through. Was that close to a real thing?
A. Yes

Q. In that experience, it was during the cataclysms, and I was responsible for getting a wise man out of the country. Was that correct?
A. Yes.

Q. Is that someone that I know in this incarnation?
A. Yes.

Q. Can you tell me who that is?
A. Leah (very slow movement of the disk, and Leah opined that it was going to give us the answer) (I knew that it was going to be her)

Q. I viewed an incident where I fell and broke my back, and was taken up into a craft and repaired. Is that accurate?
A. Yes

Q. So am I playing the same kind of role this time around?
A. ?

Q. Of course I feel like I have a role as Leah's protector, and I don't have a problem with that. Is that the case?
A. Maybe

Q. So, this role that I am playing in this lifetime, and the world facing certain Earth changes, cataclysms, Ascension; is this a continuation of that same energy this time around?
A. Seems to be the same story of human growth.

Well, I had never expected that Leah would have turned out to be the wise old man, but as soon as I asked the question, and before the cursor began its movement to answer, I knew what it was going to say. The odd thing that struck me in that answer was that Leah is certainly an innocent in this lifetime, and that may be the single most important factor in her manifesting the channel that I have no doubt she is in this board endeavor. I put that little tidbit in the back of my mind to ask about in a future session, and my feeling is that it is exactly that innocence factor, her channel, in combination, that may have been the attributes required of the individual that would set the timbre of this new community.

The Atlantean drama as a story of human growth, if believed, is definitely playing itself out again in the particulars evidenced everywhere on a global level. It would seem that the same sociopaths and psychopaths who controlled the fate of the world at the time of the Atlantean cataclysms are back in their familiar roles as purveyors of death and social insanity. People still march to the polls to make their choice for who will be the next most likely candidate to officiate over the maddening rush in the creation of more debt, more wars, more social instability, more lies, more fascist ideologies to be consumed by the masses, and to collect a peace prize in the process.

People still eat this stuff up while they are distracted by the next scandal, the next sports event, the next terrorist attack or whatever new drama can be dreamed up for mass consumption. It had to have been exactly like this in the failing Atlantis, changing the names and particulars to suit the age. Taylor Caldwell, who is well-known for her historic novels, stunned her publishing uncle when she wrote a masterful novel on Atlantis at twelve years of age. *The Romance of Atlantis* was met with the suspicion that it was likely plagiarized, being so masterfully written, and was not published until some fifty years later.

It had been said that Caldwell had the facility to cross the boundaries of time to obtain the material for her historic settings of the more dramatic aspects frequently ignored by academia. Her portrayal of the social miasma inflicting the Atlantean culture just prior to its demise had always intrigued me, yet I had no clue as to what that fascination could be. But the universe was about to spring yet another surprise, when we attended a gathering hosted by Leah's psychic medium friend Scot. In attendance was a woman who caught Leah's attention in the parking lot, and my own when we took our seats in the room with forty other attendees.

Whenever I glanced at this woman on the other side of the room, sitting in the front row, as were we, I saw her in some kind of headdress. After the session we headed down to refreshments and I immediately informed her that she had been a queen or a high priestess in some other life. She remarked that she had been hoping we would have been able to talk, and the three of us headed outside to a table on the porch, where we seemed to be rekindling a former relationship. Oh what a mysterious world!

Board Notes, 5-15-11

Q. My feeling was, and I'm going to modify my terminology here consistent with my learning and my higher understanding, when I say things like you guys set that up or whatever. So now when I say that I mean it in the higher sense that it could be you, it could be the Archangels, but whatever higher energies involve themselves, including our own, so was that affair last night, our being there, set up for us in that sense?
A. ?

Q. OK. Was it a part of the larger plan for us to meet Leshan/Lee Shannon?
A. Yes

Q. So in the sense of the larger plan, we were supposed to be there, and the energies created the circumstances for us to be there!
A. Yes

And a little later in that same session, because we were jumping around a lot as different subjects led one to another:

Q. (V) My observation that Leshan was a queen, and now I see that it also could have been a high priestess. Is one of those the case?
A. Yes

Q. And we had an association? That was my familiarity?
A. Yes

Q. (L) And her face was what intrigued me. I actually saw her face as I was pulling up, pulling the car up. And as it turned out she was parked next to us. So she was kind of walking and I noticed her right away, and I knew she was going there... (V) Was that an energetic attraction?
A. Yes

Q. So have Leah and I had associations with her?
A. Yes

Q. And there was a real familiarity among the three of us, wasn't there?
A. Yes

Q. So the energy... (L) She's part of our pack (laughing) (V) The energies are bringing us together with other like-minded individuals for the higher .... (he was already answering) purpose that we..
A. Yes

A few weeks later I had wanted to start exploring the Atlantean experience in more depth, and I had begun a basic list of questions to pursue. Usually, as a question is answered it leads to more questions, and in that way we can get a lot of information, if we stay on point.

Board Notes, 6-3-11

Q. So now I was going into that whole Atlantean thing because it

also hit me that we know Leah and I were there together, and we were both men, but I kept seeing Leshan in this headdress that I thought could be a queen or a priestess, but that isn't the question now. Was she also with us in that Atlantean experience?
A. She gave you permission to leave.

Q. She was a queen?
A. Yes

Q. Was she personified in Taylor Caldwell's Salustra?
A. Yes
WOW!

Q. Does she have an inkling of that?
A. No

Q. So she gave us permission to leave because of her higher spiritual understanding in spite of her queenly duties!
A. Yes. She hired you.

Q. So the military person that I was, the warrior person that I was, was I close to her in her official capacity?
A. Yes

Q. And was I captain of her palace guard, something like that?
A. No. She trusted you

Q. And is that what she was recognizing when she first made...
A. Yes

We had given her our number before we left, and I had been hoping that we might hear from her before she moved to Florida. We were really uncertain what that meeting was about, but we knew we would eventually discover the larger purpose. We did. I got a surprise phone call from Leshan one day, and invited her to spend some time the next day when Leah was off from work. As the fates would have it, one of her children developed a 24 hour flu, and she had to be home with him. I had told her I had some mind-blowing information to share, and in a follow-up e-mail to me she wondered if she could handle it. I was concerned.

Board Notes, 6-13-11

Q. Did we... was Leshan overwhelmed by our energy. I mean, aside from what she has going on in her life, was she overwhelmed by... just by the energy that was coming at her from here?
A. She is attracted but she has no clue.

Q. My feeling is that somehow we're supposed to eventually bring her up to speed, or fill her in, or acclimate her.
A. No

Q. Then...
A. Its up to her

Q. You mean she has to want to have a clue?
A. Yes

Q. Well, is this a karmic thing between us?
A. No

Q. My quandary is that if she was in this place in the Atlantean experience where she recognized wherever Leah was, and recognized that I was the appropriate person to get her [the Wise Man] out of there, then she must have been much more enlightened than she's aware of now. Is that the case?
A. No. She was acting as a higher authority

Q. In a temporal sense! Do you mean that as a queen, or in spirit? As a queen?
A. Yes

Q. OK. In the best interest of the continuity of society!
A. Yes

Q. So my role... I feel like my role was dually as a warrior/military person, but of some spiritual depth, and that was what she recognized, is that the case?
A. No

Q. It was just for my military skills?
A. Yes

Q. OK. But I feel, whether she recognized it or not, I feel like I had a much deeper spiritual nature, and...
A. Trust

Q. For her it was about trust!
A. Yes

Q. So is it that trust that she feels now?
A. Somewhat

Q. But she's just not aware of what that feeling is!
A. Yes

And I suppose that now only time will tell. She did come to sit in the garden with us the next week on Leah's day off, and it was all very familiar, very relaxed, and we all had that strong sense of recognition that requires no outward acknowledgment. I did tell her about the Atlantean experience and our various roles, and while she was blown away to some degree, she handled it well.

* * *

In a separate category, as my experience sorts the various episodes I can call my own, are mixed circumstances of visually spontaneous meditative recollections, hypnotic regressions, and hypnogogic relivings. This last category I characterize as such only because it includes an emotional element that draws one into an actual re-experience on that level, accompanied by a more certain knowing that one is fully involved with another in the deepest of relationships.

I had met Elspeth in a hotel pub where I frequently ate when I was traveling for work, and this particular lodging was a usual last-leg stop on my return trip, leaving me a short five hours from home. On this occasion she happened to be our waitress, and it became my custom to seek her out and request her service when we stayed there. Our initial meeting may have seemed to have been rather casual, but as I engaged her in conversation, it became apparent that she was enjoying my usual deeper level of subject matter and personality observations.

As it happened, Elspeth was a psychology major, and my own interest in psychology as a primary feature of our programming fascinated her. My frequent visits to the pub became a joyous fare of food, drink and conversation, such that she would spend most of her free time at our table. Then elapsed a long period of time where my travels took me to more Northerly locations, and when I finally had the opportunity to visit the pub again, she had returned to school.

I did however have her e-mail address, and her screen name was also her instant messenger handle, so as fate would have it, one night as I was logging on and off my three screen names just to keep them active, our paths crossed. She happened to be attending school not far from me, so we arranged to meet one night for dinner at a location of her choice on a more impromptu basis that would facilitate the likelihood of it happening, and we met one weekday evening just to catch up, or so I thought.

We had been e-mailing somewhat regularly once we had renewed contact, mostly on subjects related to academic matters in her study of psychology, and we would also discuss the logistics of our eventual meeting. As we got closer to that date, she said she wanted to send me a picture so I would recognize her, having not seen her in a few years, and her insisting that she had changed considerably.

When I received that picture, which she had taken on her web cam solely for the purpose of having a recent image to send to me, my first impression was that a seduction was on. The woman I saw was not only drop-dead-gorgeous, but had undoubtedly intended to own any male viewer who happened to see the picture. I had to remind myself that I was thirty-two years her senior, and that she merely looked up to me as a mentor, but there was no question in my mind that the picture was intended to seduce, and it worked.

Now I suppose that there are just a few things that need to be said about some of the more salient aspects of our relationship in order to provide some background. The first is my predilection for the programming factor as a primary tool of The Powers That Be (TPTB as they are famously known, or, as it has come to be proven in light of the mass awakening of humanity, The Powers That Were, TPTW). People who know me well understand my dedication to raising awareness of this most important social device as it plays into our enslavement, and most of those who are close to me are already fully aware of its power over the larger global society.

How this plays into my relationship with Elspeth is that it had always been a feature of our conversation, more importantly as it impacted her study of psychology as a purely academic endeavor. I was more than familiar with the academic psychology paradigm as it was promoted in universities, and my early deprogramming at eighteen included a thorough study of the subject as a means to understanding the early development of my personality, as well as the means to neutralizing it.

Another aspect of our relationship was the inclusion of the number seventeen in our birthdays, which I had always seen as the bridge between the old and the new, and which inspired me to the higher ideal of my purpose in utilizing that bridge as a tool to lift myself and others from the mire of the old paradigm. She had actually opened the door to that subject when she remarked in an e-mail how interesting my numerology was, and whereas she was an eight, and I was an eleven, I could never overlook the significance of the seventeen as a common element. This number is embodied in the Tarot card the Star, and it was about to become a significant factor in our dinner meeting.

Elspeth was to decide where our meeting would take place, as I was coming to her neck of the woods, and the night before we met she informed me that it would be Stella's, a restaurant and bar not far from her school. I immediately got the significance of the Star, and also knew she had no idea that she had chosen the place for any other reason than her familiarity with it. She had given me directions, and I had to call her twice on our cell phones when I couldn't find it. The second call she actually put the barkeep on the line with me, and I realized I was right there, but it was further back in the lot and not viewable from the road.

That should have been a sign I suppose, but if it hadn't actually registered on my way there, it became significant when I found myself somehow detoured on the way home. That turned out to be prophetic, because our relationship took unforeseeable detours after what was a dinner far beyond my expectations. When I entered the bar area where she was waiting, I was greeted by an absolutely stunning example of womanhood. At twenty-three years of age, she had blossomed and filled out in every respect, and had retained all the blond-haired, blue-eyed beauty of promise I met when she was barely of drinking age.

When I said earlier that she had intended to seduce, I had no idea that she would be dressing in the guise of a siren; a low-cut dress just short enough to set off her legs in a modest high heel. I was floored, and I told her so. We nonetheless settled down to an excellent bottle of wine and became so deeply involved in catching up on our face-to-face rekindling that before we knew it, we were being told it was closing time.

So we adjourned to my front seat, where I played and sang Sting, and we continued in the undercurrent of the sexual energy that we had both been feeling. That eventually led to a hug, which in turn led to a kiss, which in turn led to more kissing, which in its turn led to my asking myself what I was doing. It was now getting to be very late, so I excused myself, walked her to her car, and left in a daze of confused sexual reverie. Somehow I knew that I would never see her again, and I was right.

I composed a very moving poetic rendering of the feelings that had surfaced, and e-mailed it to her. We continued to exchange e-mails, and spoke a few times by phone, but I knew that it was so far beyond her experience, and that it could never possibly go anywhere. She eventually became more and more distant, and I could only wonder at that point where in history our relationship had soured, and what karma we had to work through. I posed that question one night just prior to my usual late-night meditation, and settled in to my normal posture.

Being an experienced meditator, having been introduced to the practice in my early teens, I listen to my breath and focus on the familiar sensation of the third eye, and within less than a minute I am usually *in.* As I sat enjoying the serenity of the session for only a minute or so, I suddenly realized that a scene had been playing before my mind's eye. I backed it up and replayed it, paying attention this time to the details. The number six hundred popped into my mind.

I was in the first person watching a scene that I knew was taking place in what we now call Russia, but it would not have been called that in the time frame of this event. There was snow on the ground, and we were in some kind of remote garden area of an estate. I could see that Elspeth was in a hooded cloak to the ground, and when she threw it open she was naked. I realized that I was similarly dressed, and naked, and that we were intending to play at some sexual games naked in the snow.

Suddenly there appeared a nasty looking old man who I knew to be a servant in her well-to-do household, and he announced that she would make herself available for his sexual pleasure on an ongoing basis or he would expose her to her family. I knew in an instant that he had gotten his way, and that it continued for an unknown extended time. But I never saw her again after that.

I wondered what I looked like, and found myself walking down a hallway in a home, and entered a bedroom furnished with a washstand and a mirror. I was shocked when I caught the reflection of the woman in a hooded cloak, and I knew my name to be Iyanna or Ilanna or Ivanna, or some such.

The very first regression I did with the hypnotherapist found me in the garden of what looked like a large home. She asked what the year was, and I immediately responded 1894. I realized I was a nun, probably a novitiate, and my name was Angela. I described the house, which was the convent, and went in to a large kitchen where a much older nun was cooking, and she offered me some small delicacy. I knew she was a confidant who was aware of my disenchantment with the sisterhood, and that she was sensitive and supportive, encouraging me to follow my heart. I went up the stairs and saw the layout and furnishings of the house, and my tiny room.

In the next scene I saw that I had left the convent, and was in front of another large home not unlike the convent. I was there to apply for a job as a nanny, and Elspeth and her younger brother were my charges. I had been hoping at the outset of the session that I would be given an indication of some further background on our relationship, and here it was. I hadn't been able to make any sense of what I was seeing until she appeared,

I followed our lives together, seeing that we were very close, me being her confidant, teacher and adviser, She was eventually married, and I died soon after. But in a stranger-than-strange twist of the magical reality in which we live, in one of those spontaneous glimpses of other lives in waking reality, I encountered a mature Elspeth much later in her life, living in some palatial setting in the French Mediterranean, and I was a young man. I could see that we had some close intimate relationship, but its actual nature completely eluded me. I knew that this was probably one of the World Wars, perhaps the second, and that as a member of the French underground I was killed by the Germans.

Finally, I had several fleeting glimpses of lives with her from the hypnogogic state, and then one evening I kept awakening from one of those states and seeing a parade of lives we spent together as women; some very happy, and others where she was outright abusive. This string of visions was accompanied by feelings of incredible longing, and when I finally awoke in the morning those feelings were practically gone. They disappeared entirely when I wrote my final synopsis of the relationship to Elspeth, and the energy simply came completely off.

Although this all happened years ago, I had to reconcile these experiences as I saw them in several sessions on the board. I also had to reconcile my feeling that Elspeth was a reincarnated lover who had been killed some number of years earlier, Betty Anne.

Board Notes, 6-2-11

Q. So there was a very vivid lucid dream where, in absolute darkness, Shali appeared. Either Betty Anne or Elspeth was laying dead. Shali came and picked her up and carried her into the light. Now was there a significant message there?
A. No

Q. Well there seemed to be to me!
A. Yes

Q. OK. Was that an actual event that was occurring?
A. No

Q. But there was a message there coming from my deeper self?
A. Yes

Q. So now in retrospect was the message to just let that go?
A. If you want

Q. Letting it go, I'm talking about in the sense that I was making connections between Betty Anne and Elspeth. And you understand that what I'm doing here is trying to get the other-life material. So I want to deal with it in those terms. So let me ask it this way. Do Betty Anne and Elspeth have the same significance in my relationships with them?

A. Yes

Q. OK. I did that meditation where I did the rewind, and I asked about it before but I can't find it. But in that meditation I asked to see the origin of the conflict between Elspeth and me, and was viewing that scene in a Russian lifetime. Now you already told me that I was actually seeing that somewhat accurately. Is that correct?
A. Yes

Q. 600 flashed in my mind when I was viewing that. Is that like 600 A.D., more or less?
A. Yes

Q. And then I was a woman in that lifetime and we were having a lesbian relationship!
A. Maybe

Q. Well, that's what I saw. So was I seeing that accurately?
A. Yes

Q. So there was a man who came along and caught us in the act. You know, out in the wilderness, in the snow, you know the whole scene that I saw. And the way I saw it was that this man basically went on to blackmail her, Elspeth, for sexual favors. Is that right?
A. Yes

Q. Is that man with her again in this lifetime?
A. No

Q. Then I began to see other lifetimes where I was with her, and I was a woman. These were spontaneous, and I'm going to talk about the one where, in one night, in the course of some time, in the hypnogogic state, I saw several relationships that I had with her where she was a woman and I was a woman. And I experienced this incredible longing. Was that an other-life

history for us?
A. Yes

Q. So then I did the regression sessions, where I was a nun, and you already told me that I was seeing that correctly.
A. Yes

Q. And I became... when I left the convent, I became her and her brother's nanny. Is that correct?
A. Yes

Q. Now, did we also have a sexual relationship in that lifetime?
A. No

Q. OK. That was something I was reading into it!
A. Yes

Q. But we had a very close affectionate relationship!
A. Yes

Q. So then, She went on to get married, and I died shortly after that, in that relationship!
A. Yes

Q. And then I saw that I was a young man; that is to say that I came back as a young man, and had an encounter with her from that same previous lifetime where she was an older woman. Did I see that correctly?
A. Yes

Q. And was I aware of that continuing relationship then?
A. No

Q. Was that a relationship that had a lot of sexual energy around it, but it was never consummated? (multi-part question needs simplifying) OK. Was that a relationship that had a lot of sexual energy around it?

A. Maybe

Q. Well, OK. That's what I saw, where she was a mature woman, and I was a young man, and I think she was spiritually attracted to me because I was apparently spiritually ... that I was somewhat enlightened and she was attracted to that. Was that the energy?
A. No

Q. Can you tell me what that relationship was about?
A. Your needs.

Q. I could take that a lot of ways. What, for mothering, her being a mature woman?
A. And more.

Q. Were those needs fulfilled in that relationship?
A. Yes

Q. Did I go on to... OK. Was I French?
A. Yes

Q. And I went on to die in the French underground?
A. Yes

Q. The scene that I saw where I believe we were looking out over the Mediterranean, what I believe looked like a palatial setting, was that the case?
A. ?

Q. OK. That's probably not important.
A. No

Q. There was a certain point when I came to see all this, and to realize all this, the energy just came off. Does that mean that I resolved whatever was left to be resolved there?
A. Yes

Q. Did she have things to resolve also?
A. Yes

Q. And did she?
A. Yes

Q. Did that whole thing have a positive effect on her?
A. Yes

While I'm sure there is much more to uncover there, what it led to as far as other unrealized or unintended value came only a few days later.

Board Notes, 6-9-11

Q. Those lifetimes that I saw as a woman with Elly: are those lifetimes that helped me to develop my feminine energy as it's manifesting now?
A. Yes

Q. And aside from whatever karmic things were going on there, was that the larger purpose for that?
A. No

Q. It's all developmental!
A. Yes

Q. But I'm using it in that sense now?
A. Yes

* * *

The regression sessions came about as a result of my desire to help Shali get to the bottom of her physical ailments, as I've already said. Whereas I've demonstrated the mixed-media nature of other recollections – that is, spontaneous daydreaming types of recall, hypnogogic, meditative, and regressions, in various degrees and combinations, the session I did for Shali stood alone in the sense that I never received any other information about her lives in other sojourns, or my lives with her.

I'll confess that I was somewhat disappointed in the operator as we began the induction, because I had already told her that she had taken way too long at the last session for the induction. As an experienced meditator I slipped immediately into that state where my mind was totally clear, and I was completely relaxed, even though it was winter, and the basement where the sessions were conducted was rather chilly. We agreed that she would do the elevator induction, where the subject enters an elevator, and when the operator, Barbara, announces the doors are opening, the subject has arrived at the appropriate lifetime and begins to make whatever observations present themselves in the scene.

My disappointment lies in the fact that no sooner had the doors closed than I began to perceive the scene, and had to wait a seemingly interminable length of time for her to open the doors. In contrast to the beginning of this session, I finished it with eyes wide open watching the scenes with my inner eye, and paying no notice to the fact that I was not physically there, even while I was completely aware of the basement room where the sessions were conducted. When I got to the point that I opened my eyes, Barbara became aware that I had done that, and opened her own eyes. I told her to ignore me and go back into her state.

Before the session began we talked about Shali and her life in the present. Barbara was a very sensitive seer in her own right, and informed me that she was seeing some significant event playing out around a lake. I can't say that I placed any importance in that statement beyond recognizing her natural abilities, and I more-or-less forgot about it.

Before the elevator doors opened, I was already seeing a lush countryside, and I had the impression of one-thousand as a time period. I also had begun to make out a rather large domed shaped building that may have been made of stone, and it was to this structure that I was directed when I finally exited the elevator. I found myself inside, marveling at the enormity of the dome, and the intricately constructed interior woodwork. The inside of the dome was made out to represent the starlit night sky, and what I imagined were the known constellations of the period.

Although I saw no guru type person, I sensed his presence in the place, and saw groupings of people in smaller rooms and nooks beyond the perimeter of the dome. I thought the place to be a temple of some sort. As I absorbed the scene, I suddenly found myself in an absolute void, a nothingness, where even the faculty of thought completely evaded me. I had no fear, and no other emotion. There was only this complete and total nothing. As I returned from this state I sensed this unseen entity once more, and knew he was telling me that this was the nature and scope of his power. In my naivete observing this scene, I assumed that his benevolence had intended to connect me with the unknowable Source. How wrong I was.

Board Notes, 2-16-11

Q. In the actual Shali regression, I came into that temple. Was that fairly accurate?
A. Not a temple.

Q. So, what was it?
A. House.

Q. Was my recollection of its domed shape accurate?
A. Yes.

Q. So whose house? (Leah asks if it was a palace maybe)
A. Yes
(A palace? OK)

Q. Was that in India?
A. Yes.

Q. I had the experience of being placed into what I can only call a void. Was that an accurate recollection?
A. Yes.

Q. And, I considered this person to be a guru, but who was responsible for that?
A. Mohrseqs

Q. Is that the name of a person?
A. Yes

Q. So who was that person, a guru, a wise man?
A. Not wise.

Q. Was this a negative energy that I was exposed to?
A. Yes.

Q. So how did I come to be in that place, in that palace?
A. Brought there.

Q. By whom?
A. Powerful source energy

Q. So it was a negative. Was it ultimately a positive experience for me?
A. No.

Q. Was it because I was dabbling in things I shouldn't have been dabbling in?
A. Yes.

It was here that Barbara reminded me that we were looking for Shali, and asked me to locate her. I immediately found myself in a public square of a village, a typical marketplace scene complete with all manner of display tables and kiosks with foods and other goods. After I described the scene, Barbara asked me again to locate Shali, and I walked over to a building at one edge of the square with a small courtyard entry, what looked like natural adobe style construction, and met Shali at the door.

Although she had different facial features, she still had the long black hair that I knew in the present life, and I perceived that she was a mistress, and my sister. Apparently we had some kind of spiritual connection, because I began to relate the experience in the domed structure, and asked her to accompany me there.

Perhaps that was a mistake. When we entered she asked me where this mysterious guru was, and when he didn't appear, she began to complain very loudly that this whole thing was a farce, and that I was wasting her time. People in the building looked at us in annoyance, and we left. My thought at the time was that she wasn't spiritually ready, and so nothing was to be gained.

Board Notes, continued.

Q. Did I bring Shali back there?
A. Yes.

Q. Was my take on her reaction not the correct recollection; was I wrong in how I saw her reaction to that place.
A. No.

Q. Is there any thing in that experience that would benefit me to know now?
A. No.

Well, the now moment always moves to a new point, and there were issues from that scene that I wanted to resolve, not the least of which was another strange environment where I found myself when I asked if I could have contact with Shali's guides. The place was characterized by a darkness of some amorphous quality, and populated by what seemed to be otherworldly spiritual entities. In one area I sensed these monkish beings in hooded dark robes, like what one would think of as a monks attire. When I began to inquire about Shali, I was suddenly facing a man I can only equate to a Robin Hood kind of character, and it was with him that I found myself conversing.

Following the episode with the guides, Barbara reminded me of the lake, asking: What about the lake? Go to the lake. And I found myself in a very festive scene that was being prepared for some kind of event, with a modest lake as the central feature in a dale surrounded on one side by sparse woods, and on the other by a series of gently sloping hills covered in grass. People were coming down to an area set with many tables and gayly decorated, fires being tended by servants who were preparing food for what was obviously an affair of some sort.

I had never met Shali's longtime lover from her teens, and some twenty years into her adult life, who she never married, as he was never willing to commit. But I recognized him in this scene as the intended groom, and knew that he and Shali were to be married in a ceremony to be performed at the lake's edge. I saw her approaching, carrying on about something or other having to do with the preparations not suiting her expectations, and I saw the look on the groom's face as he suddenly realized he would be committing to being in her company for years to come.

In the moment of that realization, he informed her that he was unwilling to go through with the ceremony and be stuck with an ungrateful bitch, as she had truly been known by all to have been. She flew into a rage, damning him and whomever else may have had the misfortune of attempting to console her. That was where I opened my eyes in astonishment, and went on for another fifteen minutes or so that way until I announced I was done.

I will only add that in the eyes-open state Barbara asked me to move forward to Shali's death in this lifetime, and I saw her in the hospital with her parents, sleeping under the influence of whatever drugs are used in the hospice environment. That was exactly how she died.

I can only thank her memory for the opportunity to have the personal experience of hypnotic regression that I otherwise would never have opted to pursue. I will not reveal what I learned from her guides out of respect for her memory. But I will offer that her experience with that lover in that lifetime carried forward around a thousand years later to this one, where she never married that man, and I can only hope that she is seeing the lessons of those lives in some totality in the place where I know she resides.

For those who recognize the many lives we pass in pursuing the higher understanding humans must gain through experiences such as are outlined here, these examples are only an affirmation of what you may know to be true for yourselves, even without specific memories. My intention was to demonstrate that we all possess the capacity for this higher understanding when we can step outside the conditioned program that is the paradigm, and trust in ourselves that we can develop our own higher understanding of who and what we are. We are born with far greater perceptive abilities than we have been allowed to know, and we are living in an age where we can claim them with the higher authority of the One, knowing that is the only Source.

Am I Dreaming, Have I Been Abducted, Or Both?

This is a question that may almost answer itself for the larger majority of those who are reading this at the moment. We cannot be so arrogant that we can simply explain either waking or sleeping realities with any certainty that they are as concrete or amorphous, respectively, as they may seem.

Without any notice whatsoever, this apparent waking consciousness may transport us across dimensional boundaries that defy our academic understanding. How many of us, for instance, recognize the power of daydreaming with eyes wide open, where, in spite of our awareness of the physical environment wherein the body dwells, we are able to summon infinite other inner-vision realities from the mere instigation of a thought.

Were we to consult any number of dream interpretation guides and apply the symbolic meanings of visual phenomena or social circumstances of waking reality as though we were always dreaming, we would likely discover a richness of meaning that would augment our understanding of life beyond the merely conditioned interpretation that otherwise lulls our senses. Or, put another way, are we not actually living in a dream state created by the very forces that control our perceptions from the moment we exit the womb, if not actually from the time of conception?

We are a social construct en masse, explaining away each

and every stimulus in the most convenient contexts available to us. We call them the elements of our realities, but they become something entirely different when we separate the conditioned myopia of academic explanations with the corrective lens of expansive consciousness.

Dreaming in the sleep state has survived eons of evolution to remain in spirit what it has been since the beginning of spirit's incarnations as homosapiens on the Earth plane. But it has also suffered at the hands of academia to the extent that it can be easily dismissed with such tired explanations as the spontaneous firing of neurons in the brain as the body attempts to dissipate the accumulated physical stresses of daily living.

Where Sigmund Freud may have offered the psychoanalytic value inherent in dream states, albeit in a seemingly contrived sexual context more suited to his personal idiosyncrasies, Carl Jung liberated the symbolism of dreams to be explored in more universal forms. That, in and of itself, does not conclusively define the science of dream interpretation with any finality.

We know our individuality is an expression of the larger infinite nature of the One, at least for those of us who recognize that concept. Such an idea makes dream interpretation an open-ended proposition, where we may be guided to some degree by archetypes or other forms of universal expression, but certainly not with the limitations imposed by those who may claim some specialized authority that supersedes individuation.

I can only speak to my own experience in the personal interpretation of dreaming as well as waking symbolism, the latter coming more in the nature of synchronicities as they manifest in a consistent rhythm of coinciding energies.

We are multidimensional beings, having levels of existence that defy our material understanding, even where we may have some cognizance of altered states, knowing they are representative of the vastly expansive nature of the One as it manifests in the limited understanding we have been told to expect of ourselves.

Dreaming in sleep states is only one indication of that vast environment in which we are entitled to explore our multidimensional natures, and they are only a jumping-off point if we recognize that dreaming consciousness can be united with waking consciousness. Castaneda's writings, if they say anything about our truer natures, inform us of the ideal to which persons of knowledge aspired as a matter of course in bringing the dreaming consciousness and waking consciousness together as an integrated totality of potential.

The symbols of your dreaming and waking states may have universal significance and application, and others may use those very same symbols and representations, but in your dreaming and waking states, they are yours. In the context of your personal experience they apply uniquely to you and your circumstances; to your feelings and vision.

As we navigate the expanse and merge the dimensional planes through the ever thinning veil, we will become more accustomed to the higher understanding that comes through the faith and trust in our own self-hood; through our own evolving intuitive senses.

My approach to dreaming interpretation has always been about my intuitive guidance, and if I am assisting someone else in the interpretation of their dreaming, I am opening myself to the more spontaneous interaction with their higher mind, nested in the circumstances of their lives at the moment their dreaming is speaking to them.

The purpose of this chapter is to illustrate the possibilities inherent in communicating with the higher self on the meaning and interpretation of dreams, for anyone so disposed to exploring the medium of the board, and whatever beneficent personality may manifest therein.

These are my experiences, and with Leah and others, in exploring the evolving merger of the dreaming and waking states. What there is here for the reader is only what the reader may wish to accept in his or her own experience if they choose to attempt such an endeavor in earnest and sincerity, trusting the higher guidance of intuition, and learning to distinguish whatever differences emerge between the higher and lower centers of being.

* * *

Traditional dream interpretation, if there truly is such a thing, doesn't necessarily have the universal application generally accepted among its practitioners. I doubt Joseph in Egypt was familiar with it, assuming such stories are in any sense true. We can take two dreamers who are having very similar dreams and find that the dreams are totally different in the messages they are conveying. The symbols may be archetypal in a general sense, welling up from the deeper collective unconscious of humanity, but two separate personalities leading wholly different lives with their individual challenges will use those symbols to express their own personal messages.

My very close friend JP came for an overnight visit, as I related in the *Circle of Influence* chapter, and related a dream about tsunamis that he had been having over some number of years. It was progressive in nature, always developing to a further point from one time to the next. Leah had also had a series of tsunami dreams, but the meaning in her case was far far different. This is a lesson in applying intuition to the dreaming from the circumstances of one's life, using the inner promptings of the heart as a gauge of personal meaning.

Board Notes, 5-11-11

Q. I'm just going to let... Well, I'll just pursue this first. Leah and JP have had similar tsunami dreams. (to JP) You had two tsunami dreams! (JP) I had a series of tsunami dreams. Climbing up a mountain to escape a tsunami, and in successive dreams I would make it further up until I finally reached a point where I was above the crest of the wave. (V) So you see that sequence of dreams!
A. Yes

Q. So my take on it was that it was monitoring a circumstance that he was dealing with over time, because you said (to JP) you

were trying to escape... (JP) escape the wave, because it was coming in from the ocean. (V) OK. Was that the nature of it? [JP's take on escaping]
A. No

Q. OK. So can you give us an idea of what that dream sequence was about over those many years?
A. He needs to know his place.

Q. OK. His place in what?
A. In the scheme of things

Q. (L) So would that have something to do with escaping?
A. Maybe

Q. (V) Well, he used the word escaping, and it seemed to be from the danger of the wave, but you're saying it's more... Is it more the scheme of things, and his trying to get higher up on the mountain....
A. Yes

Q. So escaping from the paradigm?
A. Yes

Q. And the program!
A. Yes

Q. And was his reaching that place on the mountain above the crest symbolic of his having done that? [exactly my point in it being a progressive monitoring dream]
A. Yes

Q. So that actually marked the closing of a chapter in his life as far as getting there?
A. Yes

Q. Now (to Leah), you had tsunami dreams. (L) And just as you

were saying that I was thinking of mine are always... I'm preparing for it, I'm running, tying myself to a tree, getting to a higher place, whatever. And the wave comes right, like you know when you're on the back and it just comes to your toes and then recedes. That's what happens. (V) So now in Leah's dream, what's that about?
A. Her place. She is protected.

Q. And that's a message that you give her frequently, that she is protected!
A. Yes

Q. So did you have another tsunami dream? (L) That's what happens. I'm all filled with the terror of it coming, along with a whole bunch of other people, and watching it just getting bigger and bigger, and know that I'm going to be under that... (V) Now, that knowing that she's protected is also contained in the statement that you are loved!
A. Yes

So, two dreams, two dreamers, same symbolism, very similar circumstances, but two very different meanings and messages directly related to the separate circumstances of their lives, and the invaluable assistance of the board in ferreting out the significance of the symbolism for each of them. This is something that needs to be kept in mind when we're approaching our own dreams, or helping others with theirs.

Following is a very long dream analysis from what was a very vivid dream for Leah, and it wasn't as scary as it was intense. The symbolism here includes that of a more universal nature, and also a more personalized symbolism in terms of a familiar person and what she represents to Leah. But the real significance here is that this could apply to practically anyone's personal life as far as the circumstances they may feel are controlling their reality, but not see the underlying issues that are affecting them on the deeper emotional levels. And while I may want to apologize for just how lengthy this becomes, the fruit that it yielded for Leah was of a monumental nature.

Board Notes, 5-27-11

OK. Leah's zodiac dream. (L) OK. Let me just make sure I have it all in my head. (She takes a moment to recall the particulars, and then):
I was a servant girl with nothing, and I remember realizing that I had to come to grips with the fact that I had nothing, and that I would never have anything. It wasn't just the fact that I didn't have anything now, it was that in my whole lifetime I would never have anything. It was just my station to be a servant, and I had to come to grips with that, and be OK with that, and I was fine with that. And then... I was in this large house and there was a man who was my master, I guess, and he was ordering me around, and I had to do things for him. (V) Was he severe? (L) *No, he wasn't severe. He was very nice. And I had to shower with him too, but it wasn't sexual. Because I had to be in there to wash him. I had to take care of him. And my biggest obstacle in that life was remembering that, like in this lifetime there's times that you don't have any money, and there's times that you do have money. It's kind of like a rollercoaster thing, and coming to grips with the fact that I never had money in that lifetime, and I never will have money in that lifetime, and that was the biggest thing about the dream.*

(V) OK. Where did the zodiac come in? (L) In the dream the guests came and I was serving them ice water, and I was putting ice in the glass, and one of the guests was my sister-in-law Robin, and she asked me to come outside, and actually she was planning to break me out of there. Like I was a prisoner, and she was... and I didn't really want to run away. We were walking and we get to this place where there were stars, and the whole thing was mapped out.. (V) The signs of the zodiac... (L) There was Taurus, and Scorpio, and the names were there, and it was a total map of the sky. And I was standing under it, and it was incredible, and I was in awe that it was all right there. And it

seemed to be like a banner across the sky. It wasn't like...

(V) Right. Which is what the zodiac is. It's like a banner; like a continuous banner. (L) I didn't know that. (V) And how did the dream end? *(L) I don't know, I guess I just woke up. It wasn't a good dream or a bad dream. (V) So that was the last scene of the dream? (L) Yes, and leaving me in awe of all that, and it was an inconsequential dream other than that it was vivid, it was very vivid.*

Q. (V) So, first of all, was this an abduction cover dream?
A. No

Q. But this was... there was a very significant message being passed there?
A. Yes

Q. Does she have an understanding about the meaning and nature of the dream beyond what she thinks she understands?
A. No

Q. Is this about her self-image?
A. Maybe

Q. Well, we've had other readings of the board sessions where it's been suggested... OK. In my mind, going back, it was about the body meme, this was about at the very beginning of your arrival here, WF, with Elise, and I was questioning the body meme, and I think it came down to her self esteem.... was that it?
A. Yes

Q. Is this dream related to that?
A. Yes

Q. So the opening scene where she's subjugated to servitude, and being told that she'll never have anything, and that this is

her station in life, is that representative of the self esteem?
A. Yes

(V to Leah) OK. Now let's explore the Robin thing. What is Robin to you in the sense that she played there. What is she to you really in terms of the role she played there. She was going to break you out. Is that her? You know: we're not going to let them do this to you! Is that her?
(L) Well, she does have a sense of family, and she is... 'no, this isn't going to happen'. (V) And you at some time had a very close relationship. (L) No, we never had a close relationship. I always worshiped her. I always thought she was funny. I liked her as a person. My mother had a hard time with her. Other people had a hard time with her.

Q. (V) So what she represents in the dream, is it how Leah felt about her, she always liked her, she worshiped her, she thought she was funny, a respect thing?
A. Yes

Q. And the family thing?
A. Yes

Q. So then does Robin represent the... (L) the mouth... (V) the energy that's going to break Leah out of that paradigm?
A. Yes

Q. Is the banner of the stars, the zodiacal banner, is that representative of the unlimited potential that she has as a cosmic entity?
A. Yes

(L) And just as I was describing the dream, the two horoscopes I said: Taurus and Scorpio. Didn't I? (V) You told me that before, but not this time. (L) Yeah, I did
[and it turns out she did] (V) But aren't you also a Scorpio rising? (L) Yes, but Robin is a Scorpio.

Q. OK. Is the significance of those signs that she is those two signs?
A. Yes

Q. OK. The significance of Scorpio rising is our outward self, our outward appearance. Is that more symbolic of what Leah needs to engage to liberate herself from the self-esteem issue?
A. Maybe

(V to Leah) Do you have thoughts on this? (L) No

Q. OK. Can you give us a sense of the directive the dream was intending to provide for her?
A. Contemplation.

Q. So she needs to contemplate on the dream!
A. Yes

Q. And obviously since this is coming from her subconscious, on some level she already gets it.
A. Yes

Q. And does she also get it just below the surface of her conscious understanding?
A. Yes

OK. We're going to work that out right now.
Q. Can we work that out right now?
A. Yes

So now, we know it's about the self esteem thing. We know that you're a Taurus and what that's all about, but that you're a Scorpio rising, like I'm a Leo rising , and Leo is my outward personality. So now take the Scorpio outward personality, the self esteem issue... and

Q. By the way, is this related to her body and the effort she's

making right now (losing weight)?
A. Yes

Q. Am I a positive influence in that?
A. Yes

Q. And is it more my body that's the positive influence?
A. Your energy

So you see the self esteem issue is connected to your body, outward appearance, Scorpio; you put that together for me. It's Scorpio, outward appearance, you.

(L) Well, I can be a bitch.... and I can be... actually, I think other people see Scorpio, but they don't ever see... Like I've had people say to me 'I thought you were blah blah blah, and then I got to know you and you're the nicest person I ever met, and I never met anybody like you, and you would do anything for me...' And I don't put that off. That is not my outward appearance.

(V) So you're saying that your outward appearance is that you're a bitch? (L) Yeah, or like a ... (V) OK. Stop.
Q. Is that the crux of the issue here?
A. Yes

Q. She's changing her physical outward appearance (losing weight) and that's related!
A. Yes

Q. So she has to change her......
(L) (gasps) I just got something! (V) go ahead (L) The more attractive I was, the more forceful that was. (V) because you had to defend yourself, you didn't like being hit on...[as she's related to me in the past] (L) And other women found me threatening, so I was even more of a bitch, because they hated me from the get-go.

Q. So are we getting to the heart of the issue now?
A. Yes

Q. OK. So has she been avoiding this more appropriate outward persona to make (L) to make people like me... (V) to make your social relationships easier!
A. Yes

OK. I don't see Robin as being social. I see Robin as being more uptight.
Q. Is Robin supposed to represent some example of what....
A. No

I didn't think so. (L) She's the mouth.
Q. Is that what she is, the mouth?
A. Yes

Q. Deliberate
A. Yes

Q. So in the sense that Robin is the mouth, and the liberator, that's something that Leah has to come more to terms with in her own personality?
A. Yes

Q. In whatever way is appropriate, she has to be more forceful outwardly?
A. Yes

Q. Because she's too easy!
A. Yes

Q. And this has to do with, for instance, her first go-round with the [an employer], where she got fired, and she would be calling up and crying, that is exactly the opposite of what this is about!
A. Yes

So let's stop now. So what kind of... (L) What I'm getting is, and see, it's coming together. It's when I'm standing confident, and in my body, and confident in my body, and the last time I was that was when I was lecturing for Weight Watchers, and I had women say to me 'I can't trust you. I can't trust what you say' (V) At Weight Watchers? (L) 'because of the way you look. And I know that's not true, and that's not fair, but that's how I feel. And I feel that you're selling me a bill of goods because of the way you look.' And like I wasn't... (V) And you would tell them that there was a time that you were... (L) It didn't matter. I had pictures to prove it, but it didn't matter. You know, because there I was, I was in my prime, I looked like that... (V) OK. Stop, stop, stop.

Q. Is this about her being able to convey authority?
A. Yes

When we're out together, like when we went to the Scot thing, did you feel energetically more comfortable, and in your place? (L) No. I never feel like I'm in a place. The only time I ever felt like I was in my place was like when I was in Weight Watchers and I would have people tell me those things, and then I would lose it. But then I had other people that supported actually how I felt. And that was good, but it was just really uncomfortable, because everywhere I went I got hit-on by men, and women hated my guts. I love women. I love relating to women. And they hated my guts. I was immediately a threat. (V) OK. So we just got to that this is about authority.

Q. This is about authority, right?
A. Yes

Q. So is it that she didn't convey authority, and so these women would challenge her. And when she was challenged she could not meet the challenge effectively?
A. Yes

Q. OK. Can you give us a little heads-up direction.... OK...
A. She recognized it

You recognized it? (L) Yes

Q. The way I just speak with authority because of how I am, and people may resent it but then other people just go like... you know, the [friends], and I know Leah recognizes that. Is that the kind of issue that we're talking about here?
A. No. It's deeper for her.

Q. And the deeper is the self esteem thing over many lifetimes?
A. Yes

Q. OK. So first she has to break the habit....!
A. Yes

Q. So that means a willful awareness, being more aware, more often, in order to be able to spot the behaviors!
A. Yes

Q. But it's not that simple because she has to know what those behaviors actually are!
A. She knows.

OK. So now you know, so what are the behaviors? (L) I know. I know the behaviors. The behaviors are that when something happens in the office, and I don't say anything, even though I know it's going to impact me in some way. I don't respect my opinion. (V) You don't want to make waves? (L) I don't want to make waves... (V) You don't want to lose your job? (L) No, it's not even about losing my job... (V) You want to be liked? (L) It's mostly about I don't want people to be uncomfortable around me. I want everybody to like me. I don't ... I have a really hard time being the antagonist.

Q. OK. Are we right there now with this?

A. Yes

OK. So now just try to imagine an acceptable way, take any circumstance — in the office is a good one because it's one you brought up, take any circumstance that might arise, where you do your typical thing... (L) OK. Today. [co-worker] was talking about 'Yeah, I'm going to be...I'm gonna leave on a ... *I'm not going to be in on Tuesday (her regular day), I'm not going to be back until the following Tuesday. So she's going to be out a week. That means possibly the Wednesday and Thursday I'll have to work, and they're my days off. Besides having hell on the days that she's supposed to be in there, so I'll probably be by myself. And then working on my days off, and then working the weekends. And it's happened before, where I have to work twelve days straight, or fourteen days straight.... (V) In the season, in the middle of... (L) In the middle of the season, and then...*

(V) OK. If it was the opposite, because [co-worker] is also a Taurus... do you know what her rising sign is? (L) No. (V) OK. If the situation was reversed... (L) I wouldn't do that... (V) OK, but if you did, what would she do? (L) Oh, she'd flip out. She wouldn't flip out on me, but she'd be ....

Q. (V) OK. Are we in the situation now where this is right down to the meat of it?
A. Yes

Q. So now the corrective measures that she would take to gradually change her personality to be more authoritative are in the kernel of this circumstance!
A. Yes

So now get to where, if you could get past all that, what would you do! Like, what did you want to say to her today? You know, it's really unfair to be sticking me at the height of the season, with working twelve fucking days straight, no day off, with all this bullshit, what was your... (L) No, because I wouldn't know what was going to happen. I wouldn't know if I was going to have to do it. It would be between her and [the boss] if she was going to be allowed.. (V) But that's not the issue. (L) No, but I would have been brought in on it, and then... because it could turn out, which it has sometimes, that I do get my days off, and they don't ask me to come in... (V) OK. Stop, stop, stop. Come on (take the disk)

Q. That's not the issue is it?
A. No

See, because you're not seeing the issue. The issue is that you would be hoping for the best under those circumstances, whereas, in the very beginning, as soon as she's contemplating that and telling you, she's asking you to make it possible.

Q. Is that what's going on there?
A. Yes

Q. See, now, of course, initially, [co-worker] would resent Leah taking a stand against that!
A. Yes

Q. But the bottom line is, that's what we're talking about, it's that she has to learn how to assert herself in circumstances like that?
A. Yes

Q. Now when I said to her from 2008 when we hooked up, that her weight is her baggage; that her weight represents her baggage, is that where we are here right now, that she's dealing with the weight thing, and now she has to deal with the baggage thing?
A. Yes

PAUSE

Q. OK, you were following the conversation in the kitchen. Are we there?
A. Yes

Q. So that is the approach that she needs to take, and that's what this dream was really all about!
A. Yes

Q. Is there anything you'd like to say about that before we bid you adieu?
A. This is good.

I concur (L) Yes, I do too. Revelations are always good.

And with that we thank you, and we bid you adieu. We love you. (L) We do love you.

Wow, that was a whole session dedicated to just one dream! But this is a scenario that was literally years in the making. What we wound up discussing in the kitchen was the way Leah could go about being more assertive without appearing to be a bitch, which is something that has to be done in little baby steps so people don't get completely turned off; so progress can be gauged as she proceeds to explore this new persona. And truly, as I know from watching her in some situations, she can be a push-over, and wind up brooding over what transpires after she's been subjugated that way.

I suppose another point to be made here is that the more we have to fall back on in terms of symbolism -- for instance, in the case of knowing your rising sign and moon, and knowing the attributes of each of those, as we did in the previous example, the more we augment our subconscious dream expression, and hence the analytical value. This could apply as well to vocational or trade terminologies, as where my strong electrical and electronic background is drawn upon to express ideas of power, or connections. But the bottom line is that it's all very personalized when it comes to what the subconscious is telling you, and figuring it all out is part of the journey.

Another of Leah's dreams involved being pregnant, and her water broke but she didn't want to be taken to the hospital to deliver the baby. Now, talk about symbolism!

Board Notes, 5-19-11

Leah's been having pregnant dreams. (to Leah) You've had three of them? (L) Yes. (V) And I said that it's about something being born, but it's not a baby.
Q. Is that right?
A. Yes

(to Leah) What was the part that you told me that I said you were resisting having the baby? You were being dragged to the hospital or something? (L) No, somebody broke my water. The water didn't break naturally. Something broke my water, and I was walking around. They did it remotely and it didn't happen naturally.
Q. (V) The symbolism there is you guys — and you know what I mean, are breaking the water of that idea?
A. Yes

So, they had to drag you to the hospital, or what? (L) My water broke so I had to go to the hospital, and I didn't want to go.
Q. So is that her resisting whatever that is that's birthing?
A. Yes

Q. Does she know what it is?
A. No

Q. Is this connected to that statement that Scot made that wherever I am she should be?
A. Yes

Q. And you already said that that was mystical!
A. Yes

Evolving The Spirit Board

Q. Now when I was talking to her tonight about the judgment thing, is that spiritual attitude about being judgmental somewhere in the crux of it?
A. No

Q. But you see where I was going with the judgmental thing!
A. Yes

Q. It is a big issue for her, isn't it?
A. Maybe

Q. Well, if she makes it a big issue, it is a big issue, and she knows she makes it a big issue, so, in that sense, is that...
A. You need to teach her to understand her place

Q. Is that about the judgment thing?
A. No

Q. About the mystical thing!
A. Yes

This turned out to be one of those hot pursuits that led into other whole areas, and it was only after the break that we came back to the issue of her unwanted pregnancy, and what it actually all meant in the dream scape.

Q. Her pregnant dreams, we never got to what it really is, and apparently she's birthing something. Do we really need to know what it is she's birthing. Is there something we have to pursue, or it's just going to birth itself? Do we have to know anything more about it?
A. No

Q. Because it's just going to birth itself.
A. Yes

So should we have been disappointed at that result? I don't

think so, and we really weren't at all. Sometimes you just have to go with the fact that on deeper levels you're evolving things that will have some significance later on, and you're more-or-less being given a heads-up to alert you to it. When it comes, it may make perfect sense, or you may never know when it appears that it was related to something that had been foretold in the dream state. But I suspect it has a lot to do with her healing abilities, and the fear she has around just coming out and *being* a healer.

Over two months after the *pregnant dream*, she told me about a dream where someone was dying of cancer in a hospital. The woman was alone in her hospital room, and Leah could see the cancer in her body as black specks, which she merely swept out with movements of her hand, and it was gone. Soon after, the woman's family came to visit, and they brought with them gifts of cancer. Leah could clearly see the cancer attaching itself to the woman's body as each person approached, and she realized, in dreaming, that there's really a lot more to disease than what we may think, which she already knew in her waking state.

It happened that we were doing a session that day, and immediately that we touched the disk it began circling with energy; very unusual for the beginning of a session.

Board Notes, 7-27-11

Q. Hello? (disk begins circling all over, Leah remarks her energy is out there)
A. Hello

Q. And who do we have with us this afternoon
A. WF

Q. Thank you. Was all that energy in the opening about her having to settle down?
A. Yes

Q. Thank you. Is there anything you'd like to impart before we begin?
A. The energy

Q. And that's her personal energy!
A. Yes

Q. Did that have something to do with her healing cancer dream?
A. Yes

Q. Because she's building the energy for things like that!
A. Yes

Q. And was that the message of that dream?
A. Yes. She needs to find the courage.

Q. And that will come by taking small steps?
A. Yes

Q. Well that's nice to know. (L) Yeah, baby stepping. (V) Well, that's a good thing. Anything else on that or should we move on?
A. OK (gets a laugh from us)

So, are these two dreams unrelated? This is where one's intuition is the best guide. I only know from my long insights into Leah's deeper aspects, both from the time we met forty years past, and from what I immediately recognized upon our reacquaintance, that the spiritual being who was lost in dogmatic pronouncements of what was acceptable would find her own way to express the Spirit in its most loving forms.

As I was writing this, and asking her for clarification, she related a story from her late teens, when she had learned to read playing cards. Someone asked her to read cards at a party for entertainment, and a woman insisted on being first. Shortly after she began to lay out the cards, she informed the woman that something was wrong with her baby, that he couldn't hear, and that he should be taken to the doctor. This had nothing to do with the cards, but Leah felt terribly guilty that she had told the woman this, without any authority. Some months later she was informed by the cousin who had hosted the party that the woman had taken the child to the doctor out of fear, and discovered that his ears were completely clogged, and in fact he couldn't hear at all.

So Leah's uncertainty about being a healer has been following her for years, literally, and in spite of the fact that she's been a Reiki practitioner for several of those years, albeit a very reluctant one. So dreaming will be to the dreamer whatever the dreamer allows it to be, but it is only through familiarizing oneself with the tools of dream interpretation, in this case the higher self manifesting through the board, that the full benefit will be realized.

My own dreams have seemed easier to interpret, and maybe because I've been at it for a long time. Nevertheless, there is a beneficial aspect of the board's availability even for me. The following dream involved people I worked with in the trades, and that loaned a great deal of weight in the tone of the content.

Board Notes, 5-15-11

Q. OK. My dream last night was about working, but not strictly about working; renovating a prison building. My cousin Tony, his son Tony, Steve, Dave. Was there some meaning that I was to be getting from that?
A. Yes

Q. OK. And did... because I'm not going to ask you to just tell me what it was. I know we don't work that way. Was that more about my insecurities about not having income? (because the economy had dried up, and with it, any prospects for work)
A. Maybe

Q. Well, you know that I haven't reconciled that yet!
A. Yes

Q. And it was... OK. Was there a significance to renovating a prison for residential purposes, or commercial purposes; in other words, it wasn't going to be a prison anymore. Is that what I was getting from that?
A. Yes

Q. Is this about converting the prison of my mind?
A. Yes

Q. So the people that were there with me were all related to renovating!
A. Yes

Q. So my getting all of that is getting enough from it, and that's all that was intended to be gotten from it?
A. Yes. No more prison.

Q. In the metaphorical sense!
A. Yes

Q. So you see what I'm doing with these board sessions [on dreaming] and relating them to events in our lives. So is that a productive pursuit?
A. Yes (immediate, emphatic, and before I finished asking)

Other dreams involve doing some research and then coming back to them, if you're that motivated to understand them. It also seems that Leah and I have dreams that relate back to each other. She dreamed that there were natural disasters all over the place, and that there were also huge underground explosions at the same time. I had a lot of it already when she told me.

Board Notes, 6-23-11

Q. OK. The next dream is the explosions underground. Is that dream prescient?
A. Yes

Q. Are these underground explosions the result of natural disasters?
A. Yes

Q. OK. But are they more, I suspect like rupturing gas lines and things like that. Like our technology exploding as a result of natural disasters?
A. Yes

Q. And was the purpose of that dream to alert her for her safety?
A. No.

Q. She was just keyed into that energy and saw it!
A. Yes

(L) And the feeling that I had during that whole thing was that the whole world is a land mine. Like that same feeling I have when I'm in an airplane. There's nothing you can do because things are totally out of your control and there isn't anything you can do. I had such an eerie feeling of calmness during that dream. You would think it was a nightmare and I would be able to wake up. (V) But you transcended the fear is what you're saying. (L) Well I was feeling, and listening to other people's fear, and my rational thought was that it was like a land mine. Like you can't... There isn't a place where you can be safe, because at any time and in any place, from underneath where you can't even tell could explode right out from underneath you.

Q. (V) So that feeling that she's describing, is that transcendence?
A. Yes

Q. So what she got from that dream was a different way of dealing with the circumstances where she may have previously been fearful, she's overcoming fear. She's transcending fear!

A. Yes

Q. Was that at least one purpose of that dream?
A. Yes
(L) To show me that I could.

Then I had a dream where there were swarms of cabbage moths

Board Notes, 7-6-11

Q. Did I dream swarms of cabbage moths?
A. Yes

Q. And that's my own recollection. Now is there some significance to that if I pursue it?
A. Yes

Q. I normally see them as being predatory in terms of what they can do to the brassicas: cabbage, cauliflower, those things. Is that the direction of the significance?
A. No. What benefit?

Q. Are they pollinators?
A. ?

Q. So I should investigate that?
A. Yes

So I did some investigating and came back a few days later understanding what the relationship was with the cabbage moths.

Board Notes, 7-8-11

Q. OK. The swarming cabbage moths, you see where I've gone with that!

A. Yes

Q. So I'm looking at it, because I realize now that cabbage moths do pollinate...
A. Yes

Q. And the things that they do pollinate are in the nature of things that are geared towards natural reclamation...
A. Yes

Q. So swarming cabbage moths, because I've seen reclamation, and you know I admire that (L) What is that? (V) I'll tell you in a minute. I admire nature's ability to do that, yes?
A. Yes

Q. So swarming cabbage moths is prolific reclamation!
A. Yes

Q. And this would be after what Leah dreamed about the drastic Earth changes that are going to be coming about.
A. Yes

Q. OK. is that the interaction of our combined energies?
A. Yes

Q. So we were just reviewing all that. This is our combined energies working together again?
A. Yes
(to Leah) Your explosion dreams were about the system being taken apart, and my swarming cabbage moths were about the Earth reclaiming its energies after that. And that's our energy working together. (L) OK (V) Do you see that? (L) Yes (V) Us seeing the taking apart... this is Shiva and Krishna. The destroyer and rebuilder.

Q. Is that a great analogy?
A. Yes

Evolving The Spirit Board

That pairing of dreams really describes our soul mate relationship as it crosses many of the traditional boundaries we are conditioned to accept about our roles in relationships. Isn't this more true as the patriarchy falls apart at the seams, becoming more desperate to maintain control and confuse sexual/gender energies to delay the outcome? This example seems to have been instigated externally, from the hypnogogic state, during a nap, and is all about the patriarchy, the feminine, and my own role in bringing about the balance.

Board Notes, 5-8-11

Q. The vision I had today during my nap, the woman sitting on a bench crying, I couldn't see her face. She was leaning forward. There was a little black girl on the same bench, crying and or creating other distractions, and there was another girl to my left, in maybe a booth. At some point a man came and sat on the bench facing that woman, and I didn't see his face either. Was there some significance to that vision?
A. Yes

Q. Can you give me an idea... (L)Does he know the women that were crying?
A. No (unstated, but a best guess)

Q. (L) do they represent women, in general, or what was your feeling? (V) Well, is there something I was supposed to be getting from that vision?
A. Yes

Q. And the characters were representative, symbolic. OK, my feeling is that it was about women in general. That the little black girl growing up knowing already that it was about oppression, learning her place. And then the white girl to my left, I might have seen her face...I saw the little black girl's face, and then the woman. So was this about women?
A. Yes

Q. And the man seemed to be giving comfort to the women. Was that what I was supposed to be seeing there?
A. The man was you
The man was me. That's what I thought.

Q. So that's symbolically about my role with and for the Feminine!
A. Yes

Q. Was that coming from outside?
A. Yes

Apparently Leah and I were more bound-up in the purpose of our relationship than we first realized, but it reached a point that we had to consider that there was much more to it. it is in this next section that we were really apprised of the multidimensional aspects, literally.

* * *

The abduction phenomena, in their many manifestations, seem to have reached a level of acceptability where the denial of such possibilities has become a remnant of the old paradigm as we catapult our awareness into the far reaches of the galaxy, and beyond. Thirty years ago any mention of aliens, let alone abduction, drew jeers and criticisms from both the halls of academia and the public at large. In fact, it seems that we owe our slow crawl through evolution in the present day to the stifling influence of the academic limitations of institutions of higher education. Consider, for instance, that for some four or five years after the Wright Brothers made their first flight, when others were duplicating their results, universities were still insisting that human flight was impossible.

Not sixty years later we had placed humans into orbit, and instigated the imaginations of countless scientists to abandon the limitations of academia, even where they had come through that system to earn degrees in the very subjects they were now challenging.

Today we see youtube videos of unidentified flying objects of every size and shape, performing feats of maneuverability that defy our restrictive entrenched physics, while we rely on the most primitive forms of energy generation that serve only the interests of those who have the most to gain from their proliferation. Now that is a statement I am growing tired of making, but one that must of necessity be repeated until we identify those interests as the impediment they are to our evolution.

Unfortunately, the most highly reported cases of abduction are of the nastier variety, where typically a group of small grey aliens invade the bedrooms of their unwilling victims and transport them through the walls on beams of light, and then up into waiting ships, where all manner of heinous examinations and experiments are performed.

In many of those cases there are other characters involved, as for instance taller greys, or Nordic types, sometimes the occasional reptilian or insectoid being, but the subject is usually forced to participate in every aspect of the circumstances in which he finds himself. Another variation involves the automobile traveler who sees mysterious lights in the sky, and then finds herself back in her vehicle hours later, with no conscious awareness of where the missing time has gone.

Were it not for the work of such reputable psychologists as Harvard's John Mack, or Temple University's David Jacobs, we may never have reached the level of acceptance we currently enjoy for the phenomena, yet it's hardly mainstream fare at this point. So we should not be surprised that there are other levels of the abduction experience, and it is not always of the sinister variety which is now so common in the reportage. We are most frequently given the impression that the singular purpose for these insinuations into our lives has something to do with DNA extraction, sometimes sexual mating for that same purpose, and more rarely the meeting of parent and alien hybrid offspring in some kind of bonding ritual.

There is also a basic assumption that on some level or

another, abductees have agreed to participate, which led John Mack to coin the term *experiencers*, giving it somewhat of an element of willingness. In fact, there are many reports indicating that one might terminate the ongoing experience by simply opting out. However one may view the experience, there has been very little ever said, until more recently, about astral abductions, and it seems these are more frequent than the reportage would allow.

My personal experience in multidimensional states allows for far more diversity of events in the nature of interacting with other entities than is typical, and certainly more than I've been able to corroborate. I have also had at least a dozen sightings, several of them being the more up-close-and-personal variety, about which I was able to inquire at the board. For instance, in the late eighties I lived with my wife and children on a property surrounded on three sides by forest, which also happened to be on the flight path of a major Air Force base in Southern New Jersey. From our bed we could look through a large palladian window and see aircraft departing at some significant altitude, the base being some many miles distant.

One evening after we had finished a late love-making session, I noticed very bright lights on a low flying craft, both of which aspects were unusual. As we watched it I realized that it was approaching so slowly that it could not have been a fixed wing aircraft, and that it was way too large for a helicopter of any sort. As it continued in its approach I noticed red and green lights, and realized there was no sound whatsoever. I looked at the clock, being aware that this might evolve into a missing time scenario. When it was almost directly overhead I could make out the triangle shape, and hear a very mild, high-pitched, multi-frequency hum. When it moved over head I rushed to the closest side window, and then to another, finally running outside, naked, all within seconds, and it was gone.

I had always wondered: what the hell was *that* about? But more recently, we had been doing a session, and during a break I went out for a cigarette. What happened was just too freaky to have been what it appeared to be, and I knew it. When we returned to the session, I asked about it, and that led to the earlier example with the triangle craft.

Board Notes, 2-9-11

The night was one of those totally clear, unlimited visibility skies that you can't take your eyes from. There were no clouds anywhere. As I smoked, I saw an unusually low altitude cloud just slowly cruising from behind the house at my back, continuing across the sky. It was just too unusual to ignore, and my immediate feeling was that it had to be a cloaked craft. It had a more solid central mass, and wispy tentacles streaming off. I thought to call Leah to see it, but when I put my head in the door I heard her rummaging around upstairs, so I passed and went back to the visuals. I watched it pass and begin to disintegrate at the edges before I lost it behind the trees, and went inside.

Q. That low cloud I saw earlier, was there some significance?
A. Maybe

Q. Was it just a cloud?
A. No

Q. Was it some type of craft?
A. Yes

Q. Was I supposed to see it?
A. Yes

Q. Was it friendly?
A. Yes

Q. Was it intended as an affirmation?
A. Yes

Q. What was the message?

A. You are not alone.

Q. Who were they?
A. Protectors.

Q. The craft Susan and I saw on Broad La. [in the 80s], were we intended to see that?
A. Maybe

Q. Was it intended for me to see?
A. Yes

Q. Were they also protectors?
A. Yes

Q. What else can you tell me about that experience?
A. You were exploring.

And I had been exploring. I had met my friend JP sometime earlier in that period, and some other people who had turned me on to the larger UFO phenomenon, and I had a few sightings in the area, which was known as a relative UFO hot spot. I meditated frequently, several times a day when I could, and occasionally I would hear the bell-like sound of what I realized was the I-beam that ran the center length of the basement. Someone had told me that such a sound is related to a disturbance in the ether field caused by the emergence of a craft from other dimensions. This was also a time when I had been doing a lot of Castaneda type of gazing: shadows, forest auras, darkness, etc, and was having a lot of out-of-body adventures, accompanied by several instances of bi-location.

Dreaming and dream interpretation had been a mainstay of my life, but there was one particular astral experience that shook me to the core, because I had been sleeping soundly after one of my normal late-night, darkness-gazing meditation sessions. Suddenly I was wide awake, in the astral, sitting on the edge of my bed, my wife sleeping soundly behind me. In front of me was an entity who, to my perception, was Merlin.

I realized the next day as I analyzed this event that Merlin was my own representation of the character, whoever or whatever it was. He was tall, and somewhat elevated, so that I looked up at him at a slight angle. Communicating directly to my mind, he informed me that I was to be given information that I would use at a later time, and suddenly these strange symbols began downloading in an almost visible stream directly into my mind. I recognized these symbols years later as being ascribed to some kind of alien origin. After some minutes, though I have no idea of time, it suddenly stopped, and I was informed it was over. I awoke laying in bed as I normally slept.

I was shaken, in a cold sweat, and completely freaked out, but I maintained my cool, went to the bathroom, smoked a cigarette, and went back to sleep. No sooner had I fallen into a deep sleep than I found myself again at the edge of the bed, facing the same entity, who informed me the information was important, and that I was going to be given it again, this time in a musical format.

With that, strange musical symbols began streaming into my head, and I was at a loss to understand how I recognized them as musical, because although I had a musical education and family background, they were completely unknown to me. Just as before, the process was announced as complete, I awoke just as I had previously; cold sweats, shaken; I smoked, calmed down, and went back to sleep.

There were very few people I could tell, and it always escaped me what it had been about beyond what I had been told: that I would use the information in a future time, and I would know when. A few years later I became friendly with a remote viewer, and when I related the experience to her, she asked my permission to remote view the event. About an hour later she called and told me that the nondescript entity was amused at my characterization of it as Merlin, but informed her that there had been some DNA work done, and that was all she could get. So here was another mystery that I wanted to solve. Not so fast Luciano!

Luciano da Uno

As a prelude to the following notes, I should say that I had been in a period for six months or so prior to this download of fasting three and four days at a time, water only, meditating, gazing, OBEs, complete sexual celibacy, incredible dreamings, and many synchronicities.

Board Notes, second session, prior to taping and WF
12-15-10

Q. Do you know who the source of that download was?
A. No

Q. Do you know of the event I am speaking of?
A. Yes

Q. Do you have info?
A. Yes

Q. Do you have knowledge of the purpose?
A. Yes

Q. Can you tell me that?
A. No

Q. Can you tell me why you can't tell me that?
A. Higher purpose

Q. Can you tell me from what density it was coming?
A. 6th

Q. Was it service to others?
A. Yes

Q. Am I going to find out what that was about?
A. Yes

Q. Any time soon?

A. ?

Q. Are there others who have had that experience?
A. Yes

Q. Was that whole six months in preparation for that?
A. Yes

After we had made contact with WF, and were working with him on an ongoing basis, I wanted more on the download, and it was like pulling teeth with a doorknob and string. But as far as the free will element, it is as I've suggested, that we agree to much of this work we do, at least some number of us, and Leah and I count ourselves as among them.

Board Notes, 2-2-11

Q. All these things we're involved in, these changing times, the downloads, Cassandra, even this communication: did we agree to all of this prior to coming into this lifetime?
A. Yes.

Board Notes, 5-3-11

Q. (V) Just one more quickie (tape is running out). Have we had abduction scenarios by negative energies?
A. No

Q. So everything that's happened in that sense is positive!
A. Yes

Q. (L) As a matter of fact I've been getting feelings, like that movie we watched, was just so ridiculous, the whole negative thing about aliens [generally] was just a program, and just not true, Am I on the right track here?
A. Yes

Luciano da Uno

And on to the download, with some certainty now that the higher purpose is in more of a positive nature, and that there is an element of willingness to participate in it all.
Board Notes, sequential, with WF

2-23-11

Q. So, my seeing Merlin as the character downloading me, was that my seeing the energies influencing me at the time?
A. You and Leah have a thing for Merlin.

Much laughter at that. Leads to a long discussion about Merlin. Leah sees Dumbledor in the first Harry Potter movie and sees Merlin; I see the downloader and see Merlin.

Q. Were you (WF) my downloader?
A. No

Q. What I really want to know is who the downloader was, and how much was under the downloader's control, and how much was my energy?
A. It was the Universe.

Q. So is my imagination that active so that I could basically conjure the whole scene?
A. Yes.

Q. So this is the nature of our whole interaction with the Universe?
A. Yes.

5-8-11

Q. You know, I probably will always come back to this: the download. It actually came in two batches, the second one being musical. Am I seeing that accurately?
A. Yes

Q. OK. Obviously I didn't understand the symbolism of the first batch, but I recognized that the second batch was musical. Was it the same information given twice in different forms?
A. No

Q. What was the purpose of the musical part of it, if you can tell me?
A. Communication with your DNA

Q. So that was like an activating influence?
A. Yes

Q. And that's an influence that's increasing over time?
A. Yes

An affirmation of what my remote viewer friend got. And one more aspect before we move on. I'm sure many people have had the experience of a high-pitched frequency that seems to bypass the ears as it goes directly to the brain. I have had these all of my life, but this was the first time I've ever had the opportunity to ask about it.

Board Notes, 5-27-11

Q. So I just had one of those high-pitched downloads. I had a longer one, and then I had a short burst. I was having the idea of an opening sentence for an introduction [to this book]. Did that short burst have anything to do with that introduction?
A. No

Q. Can you tell me what that initial high-pitched download was?
A. High frequency sound to open

Q. To open other aspects of my higher attributes!
A. Yes

Q. As far as I can understand it!

Luciano da Uno

A. Yes

All of the foregoing is intended to demonstrate that we, many of us, are interacting on many multidimensional levels with entities the nature of whom we can hardly imagine. I might suggest that sixth density beings are of an angelic nature, at least in the parlance of everyday understanding, yet I hardly ascribe them to any religious significance in the traditional sense.

As we continued to explore our personal experiences, before and after our introduction to the mysterious communications of the board, we also continued to expand our personal horizons. I had been feeling that Leah and I had been involved in *training* together on an ongoing basis since our reacquaintance after forty years of separation, and that it had been taking place in other dimensions that only revealed themselves as dreams.

But there is a character to those kinds of experiences that tells one they are not dreams *per se*, but events taking place in what I prefer to call non-ordinary reality. This is one of the more significant.

In a conscious dream experience, I was undergoing some kind of training akin to what might seem like gymnastics or martial arts, but not. When it concluded, the instructor asked if there were anything I might like to do now. I requested to be taken to wherever Leah might be at the time. I was instantly at something like a Maitre D reception podium, where I was told visitors were not allowed, and immediately a second person countermanded that order and I was allowed to enter.

I could see that Leah was seated at a table in an alcove booth with two or three men. It was not her face, hair or body, but it was unmistakably her. I approached the table and she was excused by her companions to talk to me. We walked out onto a patio, and we were obviously in a high-rise building.

We talked, but I don't remember the conversation. She had no recollection of the dream when I began relating it to her, but immediately began to recall snippets and then described herself. This is what finally clued me in to the abduction aspect of our activities, and why I realized we must have agreed to it.

Board Notes, 2-9-11

Q. Is my perception of the events surrounding the training dream an accurate one?
A. Yes

Q. Was I being trained?
A. Maybe

Q. Is this somehow connected to the Download?
A. Yes

Q. Did I in fact make a visit to Leah in that dream scape?
A. Yes

Q. Why was I allowed to make that visit when it was normally not allowed?
A. She needed You.

Q. (L) Because I was fearful?
A. Yes

Q. (L) The men I was with were instructors?
A. Yes

Q. (L) Were they telling me what it was I had to do?
A. Yes.

Q. (L) And that was what made me fearful?
A. Yes

Q. And my being allowed to visit was also to reinforce our responsibility together?
A. Yes

Q. And are we fulfilling that on other levels as well?
A. Yes

Later, same session

Q, Have I been abducted?
A. Yes

Q. Some dreams are actually abductions?
A. Yes

Q. The training dream was an abduction?
A. Yes

Q. My abductions have been more of an astral nature?
A. Yes

Q. Has Leah been abducted?
A. Yes

Q. Our abductions have been more about our purpose together?
A. ?

Q. (Leah remembers that we actually first met in an abduction, with many others, sitting around together in a craft, and that we were staring at each other) Did we meet in an abduction?
A. Yes

Q. And that was Leah's joint abduction dream with other people?
A. Yes

That was Leah's mistaken interpretation of what she was recalling however, as I knew for certain that we were the twin flames, coming into conscious existence at the same time, with the same energies and purpose, however such things may transpire. That was clarified less than a week later.

Evolving The Spirit Board

Board Notes, 2-15-11

Q. I've been feeling from our re-acquaintance that we've been training together in the astral or dream state: have we?
A. Yes

Q. Was Leah's recollection of meeting me in the craft our first time together?
A. No

Q. Are we soul mates in the highest meaning of the term?
A. Yes

Q. Are we twin flames?
A. Yes

It seemed that we had been doing some significant dream work as we were navigating through the earlier board sessions, as though the forty years we had spent apart were being swept away in the energetic spiritual union we had revived, almost as though we were taking up from where we left off. Dreaming was just another level, and it came frequently.

Board Notes, 3-17-11

Q. The dream I had last week, Leah was definitely there, I'm just seeing white paper and cut flowers, are you with me on that?
A. Yes

Q. Was there something more to that than just dreaming, because it lingered before I woke up?
A. Yes

Q. Is there something you can tell me about that?
A. The flowers were life

Q. Were Leah and I actually connected at that point?
A. Yes

Q. So the flowers being life were an affirmation of our life together?
A. Yes

Q. And was that the purpose of that dreaming?
A. Yes

Q. Was it more than just dreaming, was it more like an actual event interaction?
A. Yes

Q. More like the abduction type scenario?
A. Yes

Q. But she has no recall of it?
A. No

Q. So this was more of a reinforcing event from the outside?
A. Yes

Q. For the purpose of reinforcing on other levels the nature of our relationship?
A. Yes

Q. To that extent its effects are being made?
A. Yes

Q. Is there anything else you'd like to relate about that?
A. No

As we explore the inter-relationships of dreaming and abductions, coupled with our much larger purpose in ways we don't usually consciously appreciate, however many clues we may receive, we can stumble on to any number of unexpected revelations. There was a particular spontaneous realization Leah had one night during a session where we had been discussing her art, and whether it was part of her larger purpose, when something else clicked. This is reminiscent of her *Edwina Doll* as related in the *Other Lives* chapter.

Board Notes, 5-27-11

Q. So then her art, does that have anything to do with her purpose?
A. No

Q. That's for her own expression!
A. Yes

Q. And that's a good thing!
A. Yes

Q. (L) I have a question. The realization that I had the other day when I was listening to that interview with that woman who had been abducted by aliens, and she was talking about these children that she was the mother of, and she was going into great detail about describing these babies... (V) That was Kim Carlsberg) (L) Yes. And I realized that my baby dreams, and I always said that was my art, and that was me neglecting my art, when I would see these emaciated, deformed, almost near death babies, and I would have to pick them up and nurture them and take care of them, and the urgency to make them thrive, I always considered that was because I was neglecting my art. But when I was listening to her I thought that maybe those dreams meant something else. (V) you want to know if you're interacting with children... (L) intergalactic.... (V) He knows what you mean.
A. Yes

Q. (V) Is that in an astral sense?
A. Yes

Q. Have we, either or both of us, had physical abductions?
A. Yes

Q. (L) Am I protected from the memories?
A. Yes

Q. (L) Because it would scare the crap out of me!
A. Yes

Q. (V) So then some of the training/education experiences that we remember are related to the... they could be as much the physical abductions as the astral abductions!
A. Yes

Q. (L) And some of the Earth mother, mother of all children everywhere feelings that I get.. (V) Have to do with the fact that a big part of her purpose is around children!
A. Yes

So here we are again, realizing that so much of our experience is happening on so many other levels, the nature of which usually eludes us. And I have to keep coming back to the fact that so many people are having these experiences, the memories of which trickle into their waking consciousness, or their dreaming recall is informing them, yet the meaning cannot be understood in the context of simple dream interpretation. On the other hand, I know my own personal forays into the unknown, willingly and consciously, have likely opened me to a more unusual and indescribable variety of dreaming experience that truly defies any explanation. I wasn't going to get one for this next dreaming either.

Two nights in a row I had been having the most unusual dreaming, where I seemed to have been in a completely different universe, and I don't mean that in a mere dimensional sense. I have occasionally pursued questions about the nature of other universes, believing that there are as infinite a number of universes as there are infinite numbers of anything. I would awaken with a sense of total disassociation, as if some part of me had failed to make the disconnect from the experience, such that I was still having flashes of wherever it was I had been, but no cognizable conception of its nature.

Board Notes, 6-26-11

Q. The last couple of nights, has there been any abduction experience in my dreaming?
A. Yes

Q. And my perception waking up is that I am in totally... I have been in totally different worlds, or totally different environments. I mean totally unfamiliar. Is that the case?
A. Yes

Q. OK. Can you tell me the reason for that?
A. You are [there?].

Q. Are these experiences more in the nature of higher aspects of my being, as opposed to just my waking consciousness experiencing something different? (no movement from the disk at all) OK. Are these realms higher aspects of my being that already are, and I'm basically just hooking up with it?
A. You would find it hard to understand.

That's funny, because as soon as he started I was getting that I would find it difficult to understand, and he said hard.

Q. But the way that I just said it, to the degree that I can understand, is it something similar to where we all have aspects of ourselves in a much broader plane of experience, and this is more like hooking up with other aspects of experience that are going on constantly, all the time, anyhow?
A. Maybe.

OK. We'll leave that alone for now.

Well, *Maybe* to me means keep asking, but it just so happened I had other things on my plate, that is, my list of questions to cover. I knew I'd be back to it eventually. And I did come back to it, specifically so I could put it in this chapter, because I think it might have really helped others who may have had the same kinds of experiences waking up in the morning, or even from a hypnogogic state, to understand where they had been. Have I already used the pulling teeth analogy?

Board Notes, 7-27-11

Q. OK. The two mornings I woke up from the other-world dreams, and you know I'm asking about this because I'd like to be able to resolve it for the book, can I get a little more information about that?
A. No

Q. So for the book I should just leave it that I'm not going to be given any more information.
A. Yes

I can only speculate that this is an example of a phenomenon that we can never truly understand, or that there is some element of violating our free will if we were to be told too much about it. In the speculative phenomenon department, I have to go with my feeling upon awakening that I had truly been in some other world, or perhaps simply some other density, and honestly, that is something that I am sure is way beyond our imaginations.

* * *

Leah is a great fan of the *Salusa* youtube videos, including *The Galactic Federation of Light* and others in that genre of computer-generated voices regarding the Awakening and similar aspects of the changes that are upon us on a global scale. My own familiarity with them is coincidental to my being around when she's listening, but I've picked up enough to get the gist of what they're about. I can't say that I have an opinion one way or the other. The concepts surrounding the *Salusa* videos happened to come up in two consecutive sessions. Little did we know that the subject would refer back to something seemingly unrelated that we had discussed a few weeks earlier.

Two weeks in a row, on the Thursdays that Leah would take me back to where I was staying, we saw aircraft just sitting motionless in the sky. The first was a fighter jet, probably an F-18. We were on the Atlantic City Expressway, rounding a curve, and I spotted it to the right of us through a break in the trees. Since Leah was driving, I could keep my eyes focused for its next appearance, but I alerted Leah. While I was looking I was also calculating why it would be there, thinking the Pomona Air Base, which was not far off.

The next view I had of it I was certain it hadn't moved, and wondered if it was a Harrier jet, but there was no way the profile fit. We finally hit a long clearing and there was no question the jet was not moving at all, and as we passed it, maybe several hundred yards distant, and about the same height, I continued to watch it, turning in the seat to look behind, and it stayed exactly where it was until we lost sight of it.

The next week we were on the Black Horse Pike, a four lane highway that passed through several developed areas, and a few stretches of forest lands, but traffic was moderate the entire time, as it had been last week. I caught sight of a large passenger airliner, maybe a 757 or some such, over the forest, and it seemed unusually low. I was able to maintain sight of it for at least a quarter mile or more as we approached it, and then further as we passed. it never moved. On both occasions I glanced at other cars to see if anyone else was aware, but there was no indication that they were. The following week I asked about it in a session.

Board Notes, 3-2-11

Q. OK. The biggy is twice on the way home, the hovering

aircraft. They were not aircraft, or something's going on. What's that been about?
A. (Disc moving very slowly) History will present itself. (Leah also got that in her head)

Q. Wow, what could that mean? Is this something that's happened before that's happening all over again?
A. Yes

Q. Were these legitimate very advanced technologies that we were witnessing?
A. No.

Q. Holograms?
A. Yes

Q. Were they for us?
A. Yes.

Q. Did others also witness them?
A. No.

Q. (L)Are we somehow related to those aircraft? are they supposed to jar our memories?
A. Yes

Discussion, one was a fighter aircraft, the other an airliner, like a 757. So if it's history it would be as though we are looking at them looking back into the past.
A. There is no time.

Q. So we are looking at this outside the illusion of time?
A. Yes.

Q. So at those points where we are seeing them, we have transcended the illusion?
A. Yes.

Q. Was that the lesson?
A. Yes.

Q. Were we in that space that you suggested, 'focus on today'? Because I know I was.
A. Yes

Q. (L) I think we're both in a heightened emotional state on Thursday nights. (V) Does that have anything to do with it?
A. Yes.

Q. So that's something we should meditate on, that series of incidents, that disposition, the state of transcendence?
A. Yes.

As the session was progressing through this series of questions, and afterward, I kept flashing to stories I'd heard from other eras about people being taken into craft, being saved from some catastrophe or another. At times I thought I was flashing to my own experiences, but I dismissed it as mere suggestion. Then a few weeks later the *Salusa* material came up relative to a dream that Leah had.

Board Notes, 3-22-11, with Gabriel

Leah talks about what Salusa is saying, that a lot of people are going to get sucked into the hologram and get duped (taken up in the saucers)

Q. Is that right, what Leah just said, that people are going to get sucked into the hologram?
A. Yes

(L) And my dream was that you and I were; we were sucked into the hologram, and we were duped. We went up and we were in this spacecraft, and we were duped, and we knew it.

Q. Was that the message of the two hovering aircraft (that we saw on two separate occasions on our way to take me home)?
A. Yes

Q. So that's the lesson, right?
A. Yes

Leah says that Salusa is part of the setup to dupe people, even though she loves it. She says she knew it all along from the dream (one we've talked about) and that it's still all OK.

Q. Are we being duped?
A. ?

Q. Us, in our consciousness, are we being duped?
A. You are being tested

Leah continues that in the dream we knew we had been duped, and that it was OK, and that we were in peace, and that the saga continues. This chapter is gone and the saga continues. This dream was a few weeks ago. But it doesn't have to be that way, and we're here to make sure the saga doesn't continue; to make it right. You and I can make it right for us, and that can make it right for the One, those in the One.

The next afternoon we did another session, this time with WF, and I wanted some clarification about the *being tested* remark, primarily because I had that feeling about maybe having been there, whether it was Leah's dream affecting me or whatever.

Q. Gabriel said last night in response to a question that we were being tested, but we are being tested more by ourselves in an evolutionary sense (L) well, we're learning, your question, and what led up to your question was, like I listen to Salusa, and really being, you know, I hang on the words, because I think there's somebody out there who's going to save us again. That

mentality that we have, that someone is going to save us, be it god, or the Pleiadeans, or whoever, that that could be used against us, and then I remember the dream. (V) But Salusa says that its up to us to evolve ourselves out of that mentality, and that is our real salvation. Is that the sense that we're being tested, that we (humanity) have to evolve ourselves out of that mentality that someone is going to save us?
A. Yes

(L) But they also talk about that they're going to be there with the ships, and they're going to beam us aboard, and we're all going to transcend.
Q. But we don't need to be beamed aboard craft to be saved. Is that correct?
A. Yes

Q. And the mission, our mission here, is in some sense tied to our realizing that. And when we begin...when we take up the larger mission, when the program kicks in, and we're actually out there doing what we came here to do, it will be as equal participants, not having to be saved!
A. Yes

Q. And wanting somebody to bail us out, that's the trap, right?
A. Yes

It may be apparent that all of the dreaming excerpts included here are a representative sampling of the larger body of what we've accumulated. If there is an obvious consistency, and I'll leave that to the reader's discretion, it lies in the fact that in our multidimensional levels of being we are more involved with other intelligences than we can likely imagine. I am not of the opinion that we can ever truly know their natures, or that we necessarily need to know, but more that we should try to understand the nature of what we're being exposed to, and why.

We, Leah and I, see the consistency in the totality of our experiences, in both the dreaming and live interactions -- that is, what we can only label abductions, as being intended to raise the consciousness levels on the planet, and we know that there are many many others who are voluntarily participating in no less sense that we are. This final sequence is meant to illustrate exactly that point.

Board Notes, 7-13-11

Q. OK. All those dreamings that I was getting... Well, we didn't talk about this one. All the aircraft carriers being lined up on a larger vessel, like it could have been an aircraft carrier, was that a representation of an actual event?
A. No

Q. Was it symbolic of... OK, was there the symbolism of a mother ship involved in that?
A. Yes
(L) I said that. (V) Yeah, but I didn't ask him.

Q. Was that in any sense prophetic?
A. Yes

Q. And did it involve the neutralizing of the military powers on the Earth at present?
A. Yes

Q. Was it prophetic in the sense that the present energies are leading towards?
A. Yes

Q. OK. And is this the result, at least partially, of the raising of consciousness on the planet right now?
A. Yes
And these are all clockwise yeses.

Q. Is that more in the form of encouraging me to continue putting my energy in that direction?

A. Yes

Q. OK. Now that dream, the welding community [not included here], the cabbage moths, these dreams are all related?
A. Yes

Q. And the purpose is to keep my energy focused on raising consciousness.
A. Yes

Q. OK, when you said 'you don't know how much you are needed', was that a reference to raising consciousness?
A. Yes

Q. And are we doing what we are supposed to be doing towards that end?
A. Yes

Q. OK. The circling this whole time, clockwise, means that there's more to that, that we could know!
A. You are doing fantastic.

That final line is the message from the source for everyone who knows they are involved in raising consciousness through whatever activities they may deem appropriate to the purpose. We are all evolving in leaps and bounds, and we may continue to question how we are contributing to the larger effort even as we see the power structures disintegrating, all the while wondering where it will lead. Being told that we are doing fantastic may seem to mean very little, but we need to remember our limited perspective, and maintain the faith and trust that are an integral part of our consciousness.

Dreams are another point of contact through which we can work without necessarily having a plan. Rather, they are the larger plan as we hold our intent on the vision of a brighter world, aligning our energies with each other on the plane where separation through the illusion is minimalized, and our participation in the One as a higher power infiltrating all of creation is more accessible. It's all a dream, and we are the dreamers.

Early (and later) Inanities

The earliest sessions were almost a joke, as I indicated in the introduction with the story about my deceased friend Alan showing up. It seems that it doesn't really matter what your intentions are at the beginning, you are more than likely to get choppy dialogue, strange entities, and who knows what else. We got it all. This is probably a good indication of how it usually goes from the outset for those with more serious intent, but you shouldn't be discouraged. Eventually it will come.

I always started with a list of questions, and early on I was just taking notes of the answers in whatever shortened form I could get onto paper. That didn't help the rhythm at all. So a lot of it had to be projected when I typed transcripts. But I got enough to accurately represent the dialogue. I was asking questions about people in the news and various circles of interest, and all kinds of issues, just knocking them out one, two, three, with no particular order; right off the paper I'd written them on, sometimes connecting one thing with another, but more often not.

And I'll say something here that I go into at length in the last chapter, Tapping The Toolbox, that it's quicker and easier to build a foundation for questions that can be answered Yes, No, Maybe or ?; then go for more. It may seem boring or leading, but as the reader will see, it is the most expeditious way to proceed, because you're not always going to get the kinds of answers you think you are. And even were you to receive the kinds of wordy responses you think you want, you're going to spend a lot of time and concentration following them. Keep it Simple, Stupid, my sister always says.

After the first completely disappointing session, the second session was somewhat more fruitful, though not anything to write home (or a book) about.

Board Notes, 12-15-10

Initial questioning was not recorded, so this sequence is a general reconstruction until we get to a point where notes are being taken more accurately, left hands on the planchette.

A. U have the offer! U give support to us.

Q. Are you asking for support from us?
A. Yes

Q. How may we support you?
A. By giving your heart.

Q. To whom? (Disk spiraling around the board) Are you capable of providing info?
A. Yes

Q. Information in STO & STS? (service to others, service to self)
A. Yes

Q. For what purpose?
A. Help

Q. For us or for a higher purpose?
A. Both

Q. What are we supposed to be doing? (more spiraling) Is that information available from this source? Are we on the right track in what we intend to be doing - to be an instrument of

positive influence in the evolution of society and/or ascension?
A. Yes

Q. Can you help with that?
A. Yes

Q. Who or what are you?
A. Energy

Q. From what density do you originate?
A. 6(th)

Q. Are you working with others also?
A. Yes

Q. Can I get information on my download experience?
A. Yes

Q. About the nature of that experience, not recorded, because the Disk starts spiraling again.

Q. Was this communication between us intended to commence at this time?
A. Maybe

Q. Was the Scot information correct?
A. Yes

Q. Are we intended for a larger purpose?
A. Yes

Q. Is it in our best interest to know what that is at this time?
A. No

Q. What is the best use of our combined energies?
A. Freedom

Q. Are there better vibrations on the horizon for us to be living together productively?
A. Yes

Q. What do we need to know to manifest that?
A. Be free of fear. Just go to Denver.

Q. Just Go to Denver?
A. Yes

Q. Why?
A. Others to make a plan.

Q. Are the others already an existing community?
A. No

Q. How will we find others?
A. Go to a place on a map that has a dead body.

Q. Whose dead body?
A. Thomas Hake

Q. Are we on the right track here?
A. Yes

Discussion about what the implications of that could be, supporting ourselves, income, taking a leap.

Q. Who is this entity to whom we are speaking?
A. C

Q. How do we identify you?
A. C

Q. If this is a stepping off point, what are we looking at here?
A. (Spiraling like crazy, until we let go)

Q. Are we supposed to drop everything and go to Denver?
A. No

Q. Is that Denver International Airport?
A. Yes

Q. Do we actually have to go there, or do we need to pursue info or contacts re: Denver Airport?
A. No

Q. What is the vehicle or medium through which we will make contact?
A. Facebook

Q. Is there a Facebook page for DIA?
A. No

Q. What about Denver or DIA is so important or relevant for us?
A. UR A HF

Q. We are a Higher Frequency?
A. Yes

Q. Are we moving into a more ethereal nature at present?
A. Yes

Q. So how do we use that now for practical application - if we can say that?
A. Be Real (Leah actually heard that while the Disk was spelling).

End of Session

Now you see how strange things can get. We wound up spending hours trying to chase down the name, connections with Denver International Airport (which readers may know has a story all its own), Facebook, the whole nine yards. The session had seemed to be starting off in a productive direction, then whoosh!, off into la la land. And it isn't that we didn't know what we were looking for: we did, and it was seeming to be coming in a form that we could develop, until it went south.

A few weeks later we got our first freaky discarnate entity, a hag, apparently, and broke it off quickly. The quality of the sessions had improved significantly, but we were still getting the occasional run-around, and we hadn't yet established a regular or identifiable source. It seems these discarnates always appear at the beginning of a session, to this day, although they are now usually familiars to one or the other of us. This was a genuine learning curve we were finding ourselves on.

Board Notes, 1-18-11

Q. Hello?
A. Hello

Disk is spiraling and circling

Q. Can we get some indication as to the spiraling and circling?
A. HELL

Q. What?
A. HELL

Q. Who is this source?
A. KKGGJ

Q. Is this a discarnate entity ?
A. IBHAGG

We repeat our invocation of the higher self again

What I consider to be inane in board session terms are those things that are unconnected, or inconsequential in one way or another. There were a lot of things that we may have thought to be important, and we were told that was not the case; or that they were no more than just outright distractions. Here are random session notes inquiring about public figures, all of which came after we established our reliable source. I'm leaving out most of the negatives, with three notable exceptions, the last two being deceased personalities. I've also included a favorite issue of the alternative conspiracy media sources.

Board Notes, Random

Q. Jacque Fresco - His concept of a Zeitgeist.
A. Yes

Q. Is that something we can begin building on now conceptually?
A. Yes

Q. Is he being guided by a larger hand?
A. Yes

And months later:

Q. Is the Zeitgeist movement a productive place for us to put our energies?
A. Yes (very positive movement)

Q. Like hooking up with a local chapter?
A. Yes.

Q. So there's something that we could do in connection with the Zeitgeist movement?
A. Yes.

* * *

Q. Is Obama a natural born citizen qualified to hold office of the president?
A. No

Q. Is he CIA mind control?
A. Yes

Q. Is that 4th density service to self?
A. No

Q. From what density is it?
A. 3rd

Q. Above 3rd density, are there forces acting on them whether they know it or not?
A. No

Then there's this favorite issue among the more well informed: chemtrails.

Q. Who is ultimately responsible for the chemtrail program?
A. FED

Q. Is this to any degree about mind control programs?
A. Yes

Q. Is it about Genetically Modified Foods?
A. Yes

Q. Is this about population control?
A. Yes

Q. Is this about green house gases or green house effect?
A. No

Q. Is it about staging ET events?
A. No

Q. Are the powers-that-be going to stage a false flag alien event?

A. No

Q. Will there be an alien event or disclosure?
A. No

Q. Will there be a general increase in alien visibility?
A. Yes

And later:

Q. The chemtrail thing. We've talked about the possibilities of what they're doing. But what are they trying to do that they're so intent that they will kill to protect it?
A. Kill You.

Q. Meaning us - people?
A. Yes.

Q. Is it the chemtrails themselves?
A. Maybe

Q. So, do they have some way of protecting themselves that they're not going to be killed?
A. Yes.

Q. Are the chemtrails a medium for, let's say, HAARP, and Pine Gap type of instruments?
A. Yes.

Q. So do they protect themselves electronically?
A. No.

Q. Do they protect themselves by just not using it where they are?
A. Yes.

Q. Should that be a concern of ours?

A. No.

Q. Is there off-world or alien involvement in that?
A. Yes.

* * *

Q. What can you tell us about David Icke?
A. He is a Higher Source.

* * *

Q. Ashayana Dean - what is her role in the new paradigm?
A. To guide one to the place

* * *

Q. Mary Rodwell, in her presentation of how certain alien races are assisting in our evolution, is she correct in that theory?
A. Yes

* * *

Q. Is Lucia Rene (author - Unplugging the Patriarchy) on to something?
A. Yes

Q. Is she preparing the way?
A. No

Q. What is her purpose?
A. Behind the scenes to get information

* * *

Q. The way the life of Jesus and Mary Magdalene as portrayed by Sir Laurence Gardner, is that intended to be a distraction?

A. Yes.

* * *

Q. Is the Laura Eisenhower material valid?
A. Yes.

Q. And is there a secret Mars program?
A. Yes

Q. And does the shadow government have back-engineered vehicles that are taking Earthlings there?
A. Yes.

* * *

Q. Andrew Basiago, is he relating truthful experiences?
A. Yes

Q. And of course, that's alien technology?
A. Yes.

Q. And that's the alien technology that came to the shadow government through their deals with the devil? (metaphor)
A. Yes.

* * *

Q. This may seem off the beaten path, but Martin Luther King is reputed to have had a lot of shortcomings, womanizing, etc. is that true?
A. Yes.

Q. So, was he mind-controlled?
A. No.
Q. Did he have a role to play in our social evolution in spite of those shortcomings?

A. Yes.

Q. So you can be somebody with even those serious shortcomings and still have a positive impact on society?
A. Yes.

Discussion re his love of prostitutes, and violence against them, etc.

* * *

Q. Has Osama bin Laden been dead since around 2002?
A. Yes

And that should be a representative sampling, remembering that I've left out many of the more negative examples, and that there are many many more in the hundreds of pages of session transcripts we've generated. People can take heart in knowing that public figures or any type of political or social issues can be checked out once a reliable source is established.

The Obama birth issue question was asked many months before the forged birth certificate was placed on the White House website and immediately trashed by experts in Adobe Illustrator. I was merely asking that question in relation to the growing suspicion that was everywhere evident if you had eyes and ears, and cared to know.

If I seem to be a believer in conspiracy theories, that would be mostly true, with the qualification that I investigate before forming conclusions. I definitely don't trust government on the sage advice of one Thomas Jefferson, and the present corporate entity known as the UNITED STATES is as fraudulent as any securitized mortgage I've ever seen.

I won't go into 911, because I never had to ask about something that was immediately apparent to me when I watched the first building come down, not to mention the WTC 7 demolition.

But there are some controversies about which I could never

make up my mind. The idea that Bacon was Shakespeare was always a tough call for me, so I asked.

Board Notes, 6-23-11

Q. OK. I'm still hung up about this Shakespeare shit, and it may not seem important, and it's probably not important, but I really want to know. Because it is not an unusual underground theory that Bacon was Shakespeare, so is it just coincidental that both Bacon and Shakespeare were dealing with very similar issues?
A. Yes

Q. Now Shakespeare's parents were both said to have been illiterate. Is that true?
A. No

Q. This guy came out of nowhere and supposedly left nothing. Is it true that he left nothing?
A. No

Q. So there's more to be learned about that!
A. Yes

Q. Were Shakespeare and Francis Bacon of the same energy?
A. Maybe

Q. I'm thinking in terms of the seemingly enlightened information that they were both trying to impart. So in that sense are they both of the same energy?
A. Friends

Q. Were they friends?
A. Yes

Q. But that was not well known?
A. They were part of a group

Q. So that explains it all!
A. Maybe

Q. Was Francis Bacon's oversight of the King James Bible revision intended to give that version of the bible more spiritual impact?
A. No

Q. For him it was just a job?
A. Yes

(I explain the King James bible and Bacon's life to Leah)

People like Laurence Gardner, who came on the scene as a supposed genealogist to the royal families, are almost immediately suspect for me as a simple matter of their connections to the power structures. And speaking of power structures, I had been pursuing questions about the Japanese quakes and tsunamis almost from the day it happened, but one never knows exactly how to pursue relevant questions about subjects mired in government secrecy and media propaganda. Yes, No and Maybe are the easiest answers to shoot for, but it doesn't mean they are going to satisfy your interests. Here's how I went after the quakes and tsunamis.

Board Notes, 3-23-11

Q. Some mundane world issues. I asked if HAARP was involved in the Japanese quakes, and I was told no. I didn't think to ask, was there any human involvement in the Japanese quakes and/or tsunami?
A. Maybe

Q. Were those earthquakes assisted by human intervention?
A. ?

Q. OK. Same question for the tsunamis. Were they instigated by human intervention in any sense?

A. Yes

Q. Was the Stuxnet virus involved in the Fukushima nuclear plant?
A. Maybe

Q. Has the Stuxnet virus gotten out of control to some degree?
A. No

Q. Was that created by the United States and Israel jointly?
A. Yes

Q. So, if it's not out of control, it's doing what they intended it to do?
A. Yes

Q. And they intended it to go beyond the Iranian nuclear plant?
A. Yes

Q. So, now let me ask again, in a different way. Was the Stuxnet virus effecting operations to any degree at the Fukushima plant?
A. Maybe

Q. (I explain to Leah about Stuxnet, the software, and Siemens) Do I have that right?
A. Yes

I had to come back to this many times just to try to stay abreast of all the various things I was hearing. There is a lot of information and disinformation out there, and the only way to know is to ask, if that even works all the time.

Board Notes, 6-23-11

Q. So the Fukushima, I believe it was reactor number four. It was shut down. Was a nuke set off in that one building as this one guy was theorizing?

A. No

Q. Was a nuke set off anywhere over there in any of those reactors?
A. No

Q. Was it the purpose of the tsunami to disable or destroy those reactors in order to release radiation?
A. Yes

Q. And is that what they're trying to do in Nebraska with the Missouri River?
A. Yes

Q. Is the primary purpose of this to kill human beings?
A. No

Q. Is it to disable or incapacitate the energy grid?
A. No. Business as usual.

(L) That guy said today (Sean David Morton) that they (V) They were stealing the retirement money. To cover up that theft.

Q. Was that the purpose of it in Japan?
A. Yes

Q. And is there a similar purpose to what they're doing in Nebraska?
A. Maybe.

Q. Are the marching orders for these operations coming from the very top?
A. Yes

Q. (L) And they're economic in nature? Is that what you're saying when you say business as usual?
A. Yes

Evolving The Spirit Board

Then a very strange twist, dragging the Gulf of Mexico oil disaster into the mix of the Fukushima reactor debacle, if we can call it that. This was another piece of the puzzle added by someone who had spilled the beans on the stolen retirement funds. I think it all proves that there are an extraordinary number of psychopaths in the government and business, and they don't care, because they're incapable of caring.

Board Notes, 7-27-11

Q. OK. According to Sean David Morton there was an effort to balance the energies of the planet in both the BP and Japanese events. Was there any element of truth in that?
A. Yes

Q. So TPTB are trying to put off something that would naturally be occurring?
A. No

Q. OK. It's not TPTB, it's someone else!
A. Yes

Q. And that's the alien influences!
A. Yes

Q. But they do their work through their minions in human beings!
A. No

Q. So there's more involved, and I don't really need to know that!
A. Right

And here's another rub, this idea of not being distracted, or being *of it*, simply because you're *in it*. If you don't really need to know, it's more likely than not because it's a distraction, and they're part of the program to keep people occupied with sleight of hand. The Powers That Be are master magicians when it comes to the psychospiritual resources they use against the populace: fear, religious and racial schisms, cultural wars, and the like. I am not political, but I watch the dog and pony shows they put on, and I try to inform myself to the degree that I know what's coming down the pike.

Here's what I mean by all that:

Board Notes, 6-23-11

Q. Is there any value to my understanding what's occurring in that whole situation?
A. No

Q. Because...
A. You are not of it

Q. So, insofar as transcendence, and our learning to transcend, we have to transcend this whole global situation that they are engineering?
A. Yes

Q. Now relate that to your admonition that we have to understand that the world is in trouble, is more...
A. It is

Q. But that's more on the Spiritual level!
A. Yes

Q. And that's why we shouldn't be distracted by the circumstances that TPTB create!
A. Yes

Q. So our focus has to be on Spiritual unity!
A. Yes

Just how reckless and uncaring are these people who are

busy chasing profits and power regardless of the consequences? Few people are aware of the fact that the deep reservoirs of abiotic oil that BP blew out in the Gulf of Mexico run right up under the North American continent. The pressures released in the so-called blowout of the Macondo well undermined geological structures that we can't even fathom. But TPTB can, and they know how to make things like that work for their fear and control agenda. The New Madrid fault is one of those fragile geologies that needs no more than a nudge to go off.

I had been following a lot of the alternative reportage regarding the Gulf and New Madrid. When the rains, easily manipulated by HAARP and scalar technologies, caused massive flooding around the New Madrid fault area, the Army Corp of Engineers decided to blow the Bird's Point levee, flooding 200 square miles of active farmland, destroying around 100 homes, and placing massive amounts of water tonnage over the already weakened fault.

I and others thought they had to be crazy. We know the Gulf Loop Current and Atlantic Conveyor Current have both stalled as a result of the oil, causing or contributing to Britain's and Europe's coldest winters in ages, not even considering what they've caused in the devastation from the dispersants that were banned everywhere else in the world. When the EPA told BP to stop using them, they simply said no.

Board Notes, 3-31-11

Q. OK. These rumblings that people are hearing down in Florida, is that connected with the Gulf of Mexico disaster and what I'm thinking of as the caverns being undermined?
A. Yes

Q. So is that going to negatively impact the State of Florida generally?
A. Yes

Q. Should I even bother telling my family about that?

A. ?

Q. So that's a judgment call!
A. Yes

(L) He kind of retreated a little! (V) yeah. (L) Did you ask them if they do hear it? (V) No, but I've been seeing it all over the net. People all over Florida are hearing it.

Board Notes, 5-8-11

Q. Are they actively trying to blow the New Madrid Fault?
A. (Large circling) ?

Q. Well it sure seems to me like the things they're doing are going to blow it!
A. They are crazy.

Q. And you saw that I said that today when we were walking on the track, that these people are just getting crazier and crazier!
A. Yes

Q. And to the point that they're totally out of touch with the consequences of their actions!
A. Yes

Q. Is that a good thing for us?
A. No

Q. (L) Is there anything we can do besides visioning and waiting, envisioning our new planet. Is there anything that we can do?
A. Yes

Q. (L) What is it that we can do?
A. Meditate

Q. (V) Meditate with the intention to raise the consciousness on a larger scale on the planet?
A. Yes

Q. Is the consciousness really raising significantly?
A. Yes

Q. So we just need to give it more momentum!
A. Yes

Nor is it an unreasonable stretch of the imagination to consider the totality of what is a very likely consequence of these ongoing incursions into sensitive geological systems like New Madrid. The awake, aware and informed among us recognize a pattern that can only be intended to reduce the United States to a third world country. The economy has already been completely undermined.

The major national and international banks have garnered over six hundred trillion of investment funds that they've tied up in the phony securitized mortgage investment schemes, bilking even the larger retirement investment funds. Private firms like Allstate, for one, are suing several of these banks. All that tied up investment money would otherwise be fueling the economy, and mostly small businesses where jobs are created.

These are issues that inspired me to create the board and get to the truth. I have not been disappointed, as for instance in this example. There was so much disinformation flying around about the Missouri River flooding, threatening the Fort Calhoun nuclear power plant in Nebraska because the Army Corp of engineers refused to manage the upper dams, claiming sensitive species were at risk.

This was just too obvious, and I was determined to find out. I also lumped the Monsanto GMO patent issues, and FDA corruption into the mix.

Board Notes, 8-21-11.

Q. The Nebraska Missouri River nuke plants, the floods: is that about them buying up land in the area; business as usual?
A. No

Q. No. There's something more sinister about that? (nothing) OK. They are buying up land around that flooding area, or offering to buy up land. Is that right?
A. No

Q. Is that one about killing people?
A. Misinformation

Q. Misinformation? So then there was a lot of deliberate action to cause that flooding. Is that correct?
A. Yes. People do whatever they want.

Q. But can you tell me... is this on marching orders coming directly from TPTB?
A. Yes

Q. And is it for the destructive value?
A. No

Q. Is it for the fear angle?
A. No

Q. OK. What ultimately do they expect to gain from that?
A. Money

Q. So somebody is making money off it.
A. Yes

Q. Is it the nuclear power industry?
A. Government

Q. So it will just generate a lot of spending?
A. Yes

Q. Do TPTB have the technology to neutralize radiation damage?
A. Third world

Q. So we're talking about third world countries?
A. NO

Q. (M) Making our country into a third world country? [She was actually getting that]
A. Yes

Q. And people have said that! But I was asking if in fact they do have the technology to neutralize the radiation damage!
A. Yes

Q. So they can do whatever they want with radiation, they know they can fix whatever they have to afterward?
A. Secret

Q. OK. Monsanto, the GMO patents, and the farmers lawsuits. Now I saw that guy Jonathan Emord that goes after the FDA, and that FDA lawyer just came out and told him it doesn't matter what you got from the court of appeals, we're not going to do it. So the lawsuit with the people against Monsanto, is it likely that the people will prevail?
A. Yes

Q. And is that where we are actually rallying to use our personal energies to stop these people?
A. Maybe

Q. Because we still have to depend on the courts, and even more after that!
A. Pompous assholes (I'm laughing my ass off here as I realize where he's going)

Q. And is that the courts? (still laughing the whole time)
A. Yes

This is something to consider long and hard, because this is the very foundation of what they do. We are approaching seven billion people on the planet, and the media outlets around the globe are controlled by a handful of movers and shakers. That is a fact you can verify yourself. Watch a few Jonathan Emord videos on youtube. But they don't control your mind once you've freed yourself from their psycho prisons, and they don't control a spirit board sourced into positive energies.

I would also caution for sobriety, and I don't mean staying away from alcohol: that's a personal choice, and you should know what you can handle and what it does for you. In fact, regarding alcohol, we have this treasured little ditty that I had to ask, because I challenge practically every single thing that is put out there by officialdom or academia.

Board Notes, 2-11-11

Q. (L)Was I being bombarded by psychic energy when I was awakened in the middle of the night last night?
A. Yes

Q. Was that of external origin?
A. Yes

Q. What was the source of that?
A. Lower vibrational energy

Q. Like energy vampires feeding on her?
A. Yes

Q. How does she protect herself from that?
A. Get to a place where they can't do it

Q. Go to a physical or mental place?
A. Physical

Q. So is that about here, or NJ/East Coast?

A. Yes

Q. So we wait until we leave in summer?
A. Yes

Q. Does drinking exacerbate the problem?
A. No

Q. Is alcohol a depressant?
A. No

Make of that what you will. I will qualify such statements with the fact that I am a known radically independent thinker. So you can be whatever you choose to be, but I'd rather be wrong in good company than right in the worst company, where the violent programmed automatons would surely vent their ire. Ultimately, I'm connecting the physical and the spiritual on an energetic level.

I don't follow prescriptive religions in any sense whatsoever, and I rely on my expanding consciousness to lead me to scientific ideas that are of that same expansive nature. I occasionally have the opportunity to merge the two in a single concept, as happened when I asked about the expanding Earth theory.

Board Notes, 6-23-11

Q. The expanding Earth theory sure explains a lot to me. Is that a valid expression of how it truly is?
A. If you believe that

Q. What I like about it is the conversion of energy into matter. So is that aspect of it an accurate representation?
A. Yes. That's what you are.

Laughing my ass off
Q. OK, not that it matters a whole lot, but is the core of the Earth more liquid crystal than anything?

A. Maybe

Q. When you get right down to it, it doesn't really matter what I know about it, but since I like to relate to things symbolically, is there a symbolic significance to my wanting to relate to it that way, as a liquid crystal?
A. No

Q. Isn't it significant what I understand about it in a physical sense, and how I relate to it spiritually?
A. No.

Q. The Ashayana Dean exercise that I was doing that involved aligning with the core of the Earth, was that, is that, a valuable exercise in aligning with the larger purpose?
A. Maybe

Q. Because when I asked, you did suggest a higher purpose to her being here.
A. Yes

Q. The value in that exercise is the value that I give to it?
A. Yes

Q. And in that sense, it is not value-less!
A. Right

Now that may all seem evasive: two *Maybes* and an *If you believe that*. And I'll say right here that Leah frequently gets more direct answers. The difference is that the source knows I like to work things over in my mind and really think about the implications. This surfaces even more in other chapters. I understand the inner workings of things by studying and pondering, and then let them lead me where they will, combined with other things I know that may seem related.

The expanding Earth theory explains more about crustal shifting than academia's plate theory. It implies that the Earth began more as a plasma ball accreting energy particles and converting them into matter. As the Earth continues to generate matter internally and externally, wherever the particles transition, the crust needs to give way to the additional material.

Not a very popular or well known theory, but among its protagonists it is one that lends a great deal of understanding to circumstances we're facing today, especially where the sun's activities are increasing at such an alarming rate.

Of course, I see the spiritual significance in all of these things we investigate at the board, if only in their symbolic sense. And to me it's all symbolic on some level or another. If the Earth is truly a sentient being, as per Castaneda's don Juan, many Indigenous traditions, and other cultures, than the expansiveness of the Earth is symbolic of our own expansiveness, to wherever it might ultimately lead.

I've intimated that I've been at this my whole life, and that it's been a circuitous journey. A milepost in that trail was my first LSD trip at eighteen, which I explain in more detail in another chapter. While on the deprogramming path in its aftermath, I happened on to Castaneda.

Whether this qualifies as an inanity or not, it certainly qualifies as being a little more *far out*, and is one of those more expansive expeditions into the unknown that simply jump out in the course of a session. This was during a visit from one of my closest friends, JP, who also appears in another chapter.

Board Notes, 5-10-11 (with JP)

We had been having a conversation about Robert Morning Sky's assertion that the Light and Tunnel at death are a trap to keep us on the wheel.

Q. So you heard the conversation we were having about the light, going into it, having to come out again, it being a circular path. Is that the way it is in any sense?
A. Do you really want to know?

(Hard, hard laughing from all)

Q. Well, would that relate to the Buddhist concept of being on the wheel?
A. Yes

Q. So then I can pretty much answer that myself?
A. Always

Q. So don Juan's concept of burning with the fire from within is an expression of a stream of consciousness that you can enter consciously?
A. ?

Q. If all there is, is infinite consciousness... I got a better one! I just had a realization! So you, WF, have a historical record in third density reality. And Leonardo DaVinci also had a lifetime in 15th and 16th centuries. Yet now here you [both] are in sixth density. My understanding is that the death experience takes one to fifth density. But now it seems that fifth density is where you go when you follow the light. So if you guys are in sixth density this soon after your lifetimes here, (L) That wasn't necessarily their last lifetimes (V) Well, it doesn't necessarily have to have been. OK, but here's where I'm going: so could I equate don Juan's concept of burning with the fire from within as consciously skipping fifth density and going to sixth?
A. Yes

Wow, what a realization that was! That was the answer to my question, ask yourself. (JP) But he confirmed it. (V) Yeah. See, this is what I'm saying about working for it. See, he didn't just answer my fucking question... (JP) Right, it would make it too easy. (V) Right (L) But you got it. That's why you had the realization, and that's why he wasn't gonna tell you. (V) But I'm saying they already know that that's where you can be pushed.

(L) Let me ask you this. You said that... you inferred that

Leonardo... you implied that that might have been their first reincarnation (V) No, their last. (L) Oh, OK ... (V) But I've said that any one of us, I could have an incarnation way back in the cave man era, and that could be my last incarnation as a human, and I could have my first incarnation now, and have the rest of them scattered all over time. And I've tried to get this before.

Q. Is that the actual nature of it to whatever degree we can really understand it?
A. If you say so.
(L) See, that's when he starts mocking him. (laughing)

Q. But I should be playing with these concepts in my mind...
A. Yes

Q. But this is what you did to me in the past!
A. Yes

Q. (L) Is it individual?
A. Maybe

But I think that what he's saying, because all there is, is infinite consciousness, if that's the direction an individual wants to take, and they get there, and it's a matter of their choice in taking that route, (L) But does it ultimately come to, you still have to go into the light and do your own thing. (V) No, I'm saying you by-pass that by moving your consciousness with your conscious intent to another density beyond where you would be trapped in the fifth. (L) Right. To me, like what you would say, that it all keeps going around and going around, until you recognize what it is. (V) Well, you recognize being in the human form because it's the illusion, that's what the illusion is. (L) Well, just because we recognize it as some kind of thing... (V) It's breaking the illusion.

Q. OK. Are we on the right track there?

A. Yes

(to JP) See, if you work for it you can get it! I mean, this is mind-bending shit isn't it. (Leah laughs hard at that idea) I mean this is not the kind of shit you think about all the time. (Discussion about the physical properties of the board ensues.)

Now I recognize that the preceding may be a little more *far out* than many people would want to go, and it's also coming from my own personal background. There is a good deal more of this mind-bending in the *Visit From the Archangels* and *Other Lives* chapters. But I know that many people will immediately latch on to the significance of this in terms of the evolutionary leaps and bounds we are facing with the approach of the Wave. Did I say the Wave?

* * *

OK, one more inanity of the unusual kind. For those who may not be familiar with the work of physicist Dr. Paul LaViolette and his galactic super wave theory - and it is not well known, there is a celestial phenomenon that occurs with some long-term regularity. But I'm not sure that LaViolette's work is totally in sync with the more mystical concept that is the Wave. The latter is usually associated with *Ra and the Law of One*, channeled by Carla Rueckert, Don Elkins, and Jim McCarty in the early '80s. I suggest a search to familiarize yourself if you're not already. The work deals with the seven densities and the Harvest of Souls, and that is not what you think.

Laura Knight Jadczyk's work with a sixth density group known in short as the Cs deals with the Wave, specifically, which is said to occur every 309,000 years or so. One may also search Sickscent and '*The Coming*' for a more spiritually scientific explanation. In any event, the Wave is said to initiate tremendous evolutionary change, and we are about to find ourselves facing it in the next few years. It was something I inquired about several times at the board.

Evolving The Spirit Board

Board Notes, Random

Q. What Sickscent in his Boeing Whistleblower compilation, the NASA interstellar fluff, and the Wave concept as given by the Cs through Laura have said, is that legitimate?
A. Yes

Q. And will that culminate in transition to 4th density?
A. Yes

Q. Will there be a physical pole shift?
A. No

* * *

Q. Why are TPTB building the bunkers?
A. Killer storms.

Q. Is that about CMEs (coronal mass ejections)?
A. Yes

Q. Is something else going to interfere with their plans regarding that?
A. Yes

Q. Do they know about the Wave?
A. Yes

Q. Will the Wave be their downfall?
A. Yes

Q. Is that because of their material based consciousness?
A. Yes

Q. Is that why we should just wait to see what we can do?
A. Be a part of the change.

Q. So humans are morphing with the Wave?
A. Yes.

* * *

Q. The sounds I've been hearing since before I moved from Trooper, is that tinnitus?
A. No

Q. Is it an effect of the Wave?
A. Yes

Q. Can I be meditating on that sound?
A. Yes

Q. Is that sound of an informational nature?
A. Maybe

Many people are having experiences the significance of which are difficult to fathom, and in many of those cases it's about the thinning dimensional veil that signals the approaching changes; almost as though we are being alerted to start paying more attention. It certainly is convenient to have somewhere to turn for explanations when you're facing phenomena that defy logic, even when they seem to be crossing into waking consciousness from the dream state. Leah awoke several times in the morning to a distinct sound of a door bell, but she has no door bell.

Board Notes, 2-15-11

Q. Leah keeps having these doorbell experiences waking up, and she has no doorbell. What's that all about?
A. Having expectations of future events.

Q. (L) Is it from outside of me?
A. Maybe

Q. Is it telling me something?
A. Yes

Q. That there's an opportunity coming?
A. No

Q. (V) Something more ethereal?
A. Yes

Q. (V) More in the nature of expansiveness and awareness?
A. Yes

Q. So what is it?
A. Notice of new energy

Q. (V) Related to the high pitch sounds I've been hearing?
A. Yes

Q. (V) This is evidence of the Wave?
A. Yes

There's a lot of talk out there about ascension; what it is, what it isn't. People have been focusing on what we can generally categorize as *new age* ideas however they make it into the marketplace, from whatever the source. We infrequently look behind the apparent source of information to ascertain its actual origin. One of my primary motivations in creating the board was to have a means to circumvent the influence of TPTB in their hijacking everything that could threaten their power base.

New age, as far as I'm concerned, is one of those more inconspicuous mechanisms of the power base to facilitate their control. This is the point I made in the *Introduction* about the goddess energy being hijacked and marketed as no more than a sexual distraction. The patriarchal power base simply cannot abide the resurrection of the matriarchy, and risk the ultimate restoration of a more balanced energetic paradigm.

Board Notes, 2-1-11

Q. Is the New Age Movement really TPTB highjacking the New Paradigm?
A. Yes

Q. And conflicting messages in various sources, is this the same thing?
A. Yes

Q. Will this eventually be clarified for us?
A. Yes

Being a part of the change is allowing the more ethereal presence of consciousness its rightful place in our humanness. The battle raging against that threat is mounted from the corporate sector in the form of the plethora of antipsychotic drugs that are foisted on an ever larger segment of the population, children being one of its primary targets. Genetically modified organisms introduced into the food chain are genetic poison, and seem to be aimed at derailing one of the most potent threats of ascension: DNA activation.

Board Notes, 2-23-11

Q. Genetic modifications. There's a lot of talk re ascension being about our gaining strands of DNA. Is that in fact the case?
A. Yes

Q. Are these strands already there in what they call junk DNA and...
A. Yes

Q. So, is information actually transmitted through photons to the DNA....
A. Yes

Evolving The Spirit Board

Comment that the answers are really coming fast, before I can finish a question.

Q. Ashayana Dean has Ascension happening in the time period between 2012 and 2017. Is that when we'll actually see manifestations of those changes?
A. Yes.

The comment that the answers are really coming fast is an indication of how important this series of questions is, even standing alone as they were when being asked as part of the list I always have handy, one subject usually having nothing to do with any other. Just random questions. That was how I approached the idea of distinguishing between densities and dimensions, as a random question, because some people have ascension being a movement through dimensional shifts, while others ascribe it to density shifts. I prefer the latter, although, in a sense, they are really intermingled.

Board Notes, 3-29-11

Q. So, can we speak about the densities and dimensions here with you?
A. ?

Q. OK, I'm going to. I'm just going to state my understanding and we'll pursue questions. Is that OK?
A. Yes

Q. OK. So, generally speaking, I think of the densities as a vertical ascending and descending scale, and I think of the dimensions, and this is how I explained it to Leah, I think of dimensions as a horizontal, although not strictly, more horizontal and oblique modifying aspect of the densities. So, densities are finer and denser levels of being, and dimensions are varying aspects of the densities. But densities are accessible through dimensional aspects from one level to another. Am I

close to that understanding? (L) God, you lost me!
A. Yes

Q. So, is ascension as it is coming to us in what I'll call the Wave a rising in density?
A. Yes

Does any of this mean that I know exactly what ascension is? No, and I can only speculate based on years of pursuing more ethereal paths to understanding my own higher nature. I am absolutely certain that I am only one of so many who have intentionally raised their vibrational level; who continue to do so, and who thereby raise the frequencies of so many more by virtue of their adding to the overall consciousness on the planet.

My understanding of ascension is that we will become more ethereal beings, yet still housed in physical bodies that will become less dense as a result of the shifting nature of the galactic space we will be inhabiting. There is a reference I came across many years ago in one of the *Conversations With Nostradamus* books of Dolores Cannon that only made sense to me when I began to become aware of the ascension concept.

Board Notes, 3-23-11

Q. When I was reading the earlier Dolores Cannon Nostradamus books, he talked about this whole place that the solar system was moving into, and he said that...and of course, it's not what I call it and recognize as the Wave, but he suggested that there would be such a gravitational influence, the gravitational effects... and if I'm not saying it correctly, just go with what I'm saying, would make our use of nuclear energy obsolete because it would no longer have the mass, the nuclear materials would no longer have the mass. Is that a correct characterization?
A. Yes

So where does this leave us? This is an exploration of the nature of the higher self in the context of our evolving understanding of our true nature. The Spirit Board is an external tool merely intended to supplement the internal tools that are part and parcel of our birthright. We can pursue any number of techniques to raise our frequencies as individuals as a matter of choice. This is working fine for me, thank you.

I think you get the idea. And again, this is all material that people can pursue on their own using the medium of the board. So much for inanities, but it's all immaterial if you don't have the resources to experiment. The board, which ever one you may choose, if you take that route, is only the first step. The other requirement that we found was the circle of Influence, and that was where the curve became very steep.

A Circle of Influence

Imagine the most boring, laid-back, unexpressive person you know, sit him or her down with you at the Spirit Board, and wait for the communication to begin... and wait, and wait and wait. The occasional guests we bring in to our sessions have their own energies to contribute, and their individual backgrounds in larger and more expansive respects effect the entire energy of the session on the one hand, but the expansive and cumulative nature of the board on the other.

In that sense, I suppose the board is rather more a microcosm of the larger reality, at least in my perception of the whole that we can only appreciate through the lens of our limited human understanding. So the reader will not be surprised to learn that I began to view the evolving experience of the sessions as a focal point representing that same expansive ideology that described my own personal experience, including of necessity the entire paradigm that we were exploring through our incessant questioning of practically everything under the sun, and even beyond.

What the board experience began to obviate soon after we undertook the responsibility of discovering the possible sources upon which we might rely, was that there was no escaping the fact that any source had to include our own influence as energies affecting the information we could expect to receive. So there should be no surprise that the eventual primary source entity who came into a prominent role by his eventual appearance turned out to be a familiar of mine from other sojourns.

This is where the paradigm meets the reflection of itself in the most pragmatic of terms. Indeed, when we question the very nature of our realities by attempting to devise the tools that will allow us to objectify our subjective ideologies, we will be continually testing the parameters of how we have been told it should be. We compare left-brain logical assumptions against the broader experience we are distilling from the intuitive nature of the soul in trust and faith; in a higher ideal arising from the more expansive self.

For those of a more academic nature, who will argue the futility of abandoning the time-tested proofs of the strictly logical processes that have brought humanity through thousands of years of history so successfully, I can only suggest that we have hardly questioned a paradigm whose success relies upon the perspective of the victor, writing the history of our latest war.

To be sure, the enlightened swami has attempted to redirect our energies toward an ideal embodied in the teachings of most religious institutions, but those same institutions are the first to abandon those ideals when their home country embarks on a course of war. And in truth, are we not compelled to make them the arbiters and intermediaries of the larger reality that springs from a Source to which only they can truly relate?

And if I seem to digress, I am only setting the tone for what I began to intimate in what has already been described as an evolving understanding of much larger issues as they began to emerge from our limited understanding of the complexities inherent in the potential of our very serious approach to the sessions. It eventually became a religious undertaking only in the sense that religion is a *tying back* to our One True Source. But our individual personalities were not sacrificed to some contrived notion of ritualistic propriety. So this is the exposition of the unbroken circle of purpose revealed in what became our mysterious community. And there was a lot of laughing as well.

My own disposition could hardly be considered as one devoid of left-brain thinking, even where my particular path may have led me to forsake the academic system that left me frustrated beyond measure. The programming already operating in my Irish/Italian Catholic family life had taken its toll on my creative freedom insofar as the guilt feelings that seemed to interfere in every endeavor I undertook. My father frequently expressed, in his own simple language, that I should know my station in life and stay there.

'Delusions of grandeur' were the way he chose to identify any aspirations inconsistent with his own understanding of the purpose and possibilities of what he limited to the mere accomplishment of learning a skill and making a living. One could be comfortable, as my parents certainly were, though not opulent by any means.

I may have been fortunate in being exposed to a variety of skills in my upbringing that I took for granted in my adult years, believing everyone could do the things I did, and do them better. This was my father's humbling influence, in that his own superior skills as a mechanic, about which others raved to me as bordering on the brilliant, could not be thought of as such lest he develop a big head.

That certainly didn't prevent him from being critical or intolerant when it came to his expectations for his oldest son. I was derided as being stupid, or a jackass, by my father, while my mother and teachers insisted my own brilliance was wasted in my laziness. Little did anyone know that I had been harboring an unidentifiable spiritual aspiration that became misconstrued as a desire to become a priest, since I saw no other possible outlet ..., until the smoke and mirrors of Catholicism cleared. At that point I sought other spiritual, and more mystical, interests.

Sometime in my early teens I came across the Christmas Humphreys book already mentioned, which sufficiently turned my mind to such a positive direction that I began to have a more reasonable understanding of my true potential, albeit one of isolated study, absent any friends with whom I could relate its significance.

When I met Alan Goldstein at seventeen, I was exposed to the influence of the Jewish boys, whose contrasting free-spirited ways offered me an alternative glimpse of lifestyle attitudes and choices devoid of the kinds of programming I had endured. I embraced their cultural uniqueness with relish, and went to live with Alan's family for a couple of years to escape the oppressive environment of my familial home. As I began to shake the confines of superstitious conditioning, the heaven and hell of expectations, started smoking pot, and was introduced to a wider variety of people, I was ready for more expansive forays into reality.

That ushered in the most expansive era of my life up to that time. I took LSD at a party, had a very bad initial trip, ravaged by fear, which led into a euphoric sense of extreme heightened awareness, though at that point I had never heard of such a term. Yet I finished the trip in a small inner-city courtyard cemetery completely hidden from the street, and discoursed to my friends on the meaning of life.

Some months later I began to have flashbacks, and was faced with unraveling the fear responses that I recognized as the foundation of the bad part of my first trip, now rearing its ugly head with no chemical stimulation. I was faced with undertaking the study of psychology, and when I came across Pavlov, a Bell went off in my head (pun intended). I had the flash of insight that led me to an understanding of my own conditioned responses.

What followed was a gift from the Infinite, in that I was fortunate to meet people from one stage of my life to each successive stage who contributed the next sequence of learning I needed to navigate a path to spiritual fulfillment. I never looked back except to gauge the progress I made as more and more synchronicities arranged themselves as though a cosmic hand was steering my course. And it was.

By the time I was introduced to the works of Carlos Castaneda I had consumed innumerable works of science, philosophy and literature, and developed a hunger that was so insatiable that I moved from one educational resource to the next without any thought of direction. I not only read the don Juan material, I practiced every possible maneuver I could understand from the stories and techniques related in that now-classic series, and still do to this very day.

It was while I was constructing a new self based in the movement of Spirit in my life that I met Leah, a friend of my sister's who lived in the apartment across the hall from her. I had gone to my sister's for a family event, and when our eyes made contact, it was all over. I soon found out that Leah and I were born in the same inner-city hospital, had lived our familial lives only a mile from each other, and had a bent towards things spiritual.

The big difference was that Leah was an admitted bible thumper, while I had been liberated from that paradigm to pursue a more mystical study and understanding of Spirit. Nevertheless, we attempted to reconcile our disparate views of the meaning of the Infinite, and when we could not come to any satisfactory accord, we separated on very friendly terms. She pursued the white picket fence and converted to Judaism in order to fully participate in her new husband's life, and I went on to find Spirit everywhere that I knew Spirit could be found, within and without.

The point of all the foregoing is that neither of us just wandered into the spirit board to see what we might be able to stir up. When we came back together after forty years of life experience, we had cultivated very similar attitudes and understandings of things spiritual. Although Leah was still possessed of her more Christian foundational program, and I was adverse to the restrictive concepts inherent therein as a function of the societal limitations they imposed, we saw an opportunity for growth in each the other.

It was hardly all peaches-and-cream however, as other issues came to play into the mix that was the foundation of our relationship. While I had made a successful career in the trades over the years, the work I had been doing started drying up, even to the point where more menial jobs became increasingly unavailable. My Tarot readings over some few years had been suggesting I needed to be led by the larger hand, but I simply could not let go of the control that intelligent people expect to assert in life.

Evolving The Spirit Board

Leah had always been gainfully employed in those times when her familial and marital responsibilities allowed her that freedom. Her standard of belief allowed for no possibility that anyone who wished to work would not find it somewhere or other. It was a trying time for her, not realizing that she herself was actually molding a new persona, as I had been suggesting from the time we had become reacquainted.

I recognized that she had been no less led than I had, but less familiar with the trappings of Spirit in terms of the unpredictable events that can change our perspective in a heartbeat. When circumstances placed me many hundreds of miles away, and the phone conversations became more testy, and less frequent, I knew that the pressure was about to take its toll.

The tension escalated to the point that we were no longer speaking by phone, and e-mails from me began to go unanswered more frequently. Suddenly, whatever answers did come were more and more hostile. As I contemplated the deeper nature of our true relationship, and the fact that we were so well-suited to each other on a spiritual level, it dawned on me that she was under a psychic attack. I will ask the reader to indulge this explanation without prejudice, because as we learned later, and as I briefly reflected in The Shadow Self chapter, I could not have been more correct.

Realizing what I did, I continued to send Leah e-mails of material that I knew would be of interest, mostly links to subjects that would pique her curiosity. I simply overlooked her very last reply to me, where she told me very matter-of-fact that she never wanted to speak to me again. I decided that Spirit would dictate, and Spirit was moving me to maintain a detached attitude, and continue to feed her the materials I believed would inspire her spiritually.

We hadn't seen each other since New Years Day 2010, and I hadn't spoken to her since April. Her last bitter e-mail reply to me was in early summer. Yet I persisted in the belief that she would eventually come around to see what Spirit intended, if that was truly the case. Suddenly, in mid October, when I had linked her a forum posting of a Beach Boy tune, Feel Flows, (Brian Wilson was my hero), which included the lyrics, she actually replied. I was encouraged, if cautiously. That e-mail re-opened the channels of our communication, and soon after she was visiting me on each Thursday that she attended a college class not far from where I was living at the time.

Now, that whole story may not have seemed to have any relevance to our eventual planning and constructing of a Spirit Board, but for months I had been feeling the pull to design and create such a board. I had even suggested to another very close lady friend that she think about whether or not she might be interested in operating the board with me. Surprisingly, when I suggested to Leah that we create and construct a board, she immediately concurred.

From that point on, I began taking public transportation every week to spend her two days off with her, and on one of those visits we mutually decided it was ridiculous to be living separately, and I stayed for several months. What had begun as a helter-skelter attempt to elicit information from sources we had no hope of identifying soon became an open relationship with very identifiable entities. And the individual energies influencing the board also began to make themselves more and more obvious.

At some point I had begun to favor the term gestalt as being the most appropriate description of how the energy actually manifested, because I began to become more aware of the energetic nature of the whole project. It manifested in two very simple yes-or-no questions:

Board Notes, 3-17-11

Q. So how are we interacting in the bigger picture, just by doing what we're doing?
A. Yes

Q. And somehow all of those energies form like a Gestalt, and that's the bigger picture?

A. Yes.

It soon became a common characterization, and I'm making this point now because it eventually evolved that we were utilizing the gestalt in every session without realizing it to be a controlling feature of the project. From an earlier chapter:

Board Notes, with Gabriel

Q. OK, we are beautiful. OK, so let me ask this, and I used the word the other night talking to WF, is this, just for lack of a really...because this is amorphous enough for both of us, is this a gestalt in the 'you are beautiful' gestalt, and you are beautiful is everywhere, now?
A. You are not of this world

I had walked outside earlier to smoke, and as soon as I looked at the night sky (as I always do) I was overcome with the pragmatic knowledge that I am not of this world, and even stuck my head in the door to tell Leah.
Q. And you must be aware of that realization I had stepping outside the door tonight?
A. Yes

Q. Now, are you, or other energies around us and you, feeding this in some way?
A. Yes

Q. And the feeding is the gestalt!
A. Yes

Now, it may not seem that Gabriel was acknowledging the gestalt terminology, but his answer presumed there was no question as to our having used it. As I said, it became a rather commonplace usage after its initial invocation as a descriptor of what I saw as the energetic foundation. Examples persist.

Luciano da Uno

Board Notes, Random sessions:

Q. (L) So is he (Gabriel) also one of our guardians?
A. Yes

Q. So this is...and this is my new word for it now, this whole energy gestalt!
A. Yes

* * *

Q. So this is the 'you are beautiful gestalt' pulling Mozart out of the 18th century to reinforce this energy!
A. Yes

Q. Because we just have to give up and jump into the ocean of this energy and go with it?
A. Yes

* * *

Q. Obviously his coming through the way he did had more of a spiritual intent. So there are entities with whom we've had relationships that are now, some aspect of them is now on that side, and they're just joining in this gestalt that is expressing itself now, and through us, inclusively!
A. Yes

* * *

Q. That's part of what I'm calling the gestalt!
A. Yes

Q. This gestalt resonates all the way up to where you are!

A. It's different

Q. I understand that, but what I'm saying is that in the sense of our higher selves...
A. Yes

Q. Right, and so you are our higher selves and we are you!
A. Yes

Q. And resonance is that we are all aspects of a circuit...
A. Yes

Q. and every aspect of a circuit resonates at its own resonant frequency...
A. Yes

* * *

(with Gabriel, and my daughter Gabrielle)
Q. So Teagan (my grandson) and Kris (my son) manifesting into the same gestalt, and you know this is how I've chosen to identify this; I've used it with you, and I've used it with WF, because that's how I see it, Kris and Teagan, choosing to manifest into this same gestalt, is a pattern that is being set up through this gestalt for the purpose of where we are taking this ascension energy now! (No response) You knew that was a question mark Gabriel (although I said it more as a statement) (G) I was going to say, was there a question there? (V) He knows that. He knows how I speak. (L) Something else is going to be coming.
A. It is for their growth and humanity

So I think the point should be well-taken by now, and I can be getting on to how the gestalt idea manifests in those who come to the board and bring that same energy with them as individuals, yet also demonstrate their individual energies by influencing the operation of the board. What should be apparent from what I've already revealed about my own basic nature, and my personal development from an undirected spiritually motivated youth to a purposeful adult, is the deeper issues I was exploring through the board.

Leah and I hadn't really felt we had obtained a reliable source until her daughter Elise arrived for an overnight, and wanted to inquire about her personal guides and guardians. That marked the first appearance of WF, and I consider this to be a perfect example of someone's individual energetic contribution to the gestalt. This development was somewhat confusing in its introduction, coming over a two-day period, so I'll begin with smaller snippets and build from there.

I should probably begin with the fact that it eventually surfaced in the sessions that Leah, Elise and I had shared a number of lifetimes, and all of them seemed to have had a spiritual basis. Elise is a Reiki master, teaches Qi Gong, and is heavily involved with healing and reintroducing back to the wild a variety of injured or orphaned animals that are brought to the local animal shelter where she volunteers. Whatever spiritual lives she's lived, she was manifesting that energy in this life as well. Hence her interest in identifying her personal guides and guardians.

The first day brought us an entity who was variously identified as Leo and Leonardo in answer to questions about Elise's guardians. This turned out to be an entity from sixth density who I later realized was the ascended Leonardo DaVinci, my hero. The second day the session began with the appearance of Leah's father, who had passed some many years earlier, and at the end of that dialogue we asked to be connected to our usual source (whose actual name we had only gotten the previous day).

Board Notes, 1-26-11

Q. (L) Say goodbye dad.
A. Goodbye

Evolving The Spirit Board

Q. (V) Can we have our normal 6th density contact now? Hello?
A. Hello

Q. Who do we have with us?
A. Leonardo

Q. What density are you from?
A. 6

Q. Was there more to communicate?
A. Yes

Q. Can you communicate directly?
A. Yes

Q. Give us direction on what you want to pursue?
A. Maybe

Q. When Elise got the answer it was Leo, was it one and the same?
A. Yes

Q. Are you in fact a guardian?
A. Yes

Q. Were you coming through for her?
A. Yes

Q. Can we assume that guardian angels are 6th density?
A. Yes

Q. What is it that you want me to communicate?
A. WF (our published designation of the name)

This was our introduction to the entity that from that time on became our primary contact, and if he had been with us before that time, we certainly had no knowledge of having interacted with him. When I eventually asked about the likelihood that it was Elise who had brought him to the board, months later, he quickly affirmed it.

Board Notes, 4-2-11

Q. You basically came to us, we felt, through Elise's presence here. Was it her presence that actually brought you here - and if we asked this before, I'm sorry. Was it her presence here that brought you here?
A. Yes

Q. And then it seemed like you were coming in with a Leonardo entity, is that right?
A. Yes

Q. You and he are of the same energy?
A. Yes

Q. Leonardo, that personage that you came through with, was that like you guys were running with the energy, and finally the energy was more yours than his?
A. Yes

Q. So you both have the same function in the affairs of humanity, it's more like which
one's energy is more aligned?
A. We are one

Q. But we just have the interaction of the personality energy that resonates with us?
A. Yes

A point I'd like to reinforce here is that I have frequently mentioned WF's capacity for humor, colloquialisms, and a flare for the dramatic. This is *his* personality, and that is altogether consistent with our own natural personalities as we embark on the occasional protracted discussions that may become necessary to clarify our intentions, or whatever issues may arise. We are not unlikely to resort to what some may consider as being the more crass forms of the vernacular, and it has never interrupted the flow of the board.

And Elise wasn't just bringing WF to the board as a total stranger. We all had an energy connection beyond a mere coincidental or accidental appearance. For instance, there was this innocent question for Leah:

Board Notes, 2-10-11

Q. The psychic Karen saw an American Indian around Leah. Was that WF?
A. Yes

Then there was my own past association, gradually coming out over a period of time. It started innocently enough when I was pursuing a spontaneous recollection from some years earlier of another lifetime that I'd had. I've already discussed that in the *Other Lives* chapter.

So there is a gestalt transcending the limitations we put in our linear perspective of time; the energetic influences coming through the board without our consciously willing such manifestations. As I've said elsewhere, the nature of our source is to instruct, and not simply to answer questions that we put to it/him/them. I could never have dreamed at the outset of this project that I would have come to meet the entity responsible for my heightened understanding in a lifetime lived probably two hundred or more years ago.

But there is another aspect to these energies that come to influence the board: a connection to other lifetimes among the participants. I will leave that particular theme for later discussion after some more introductions. Suffice it to say that the connections that have been tied together so far in this circle of influence have more expansive twists to take before we have begun to unravel these mysterious energies.

I've shown how Elise brought us our connection to WF, and how that connection had already existed on other levels for Leah and for me, individually. In the beginning of our sessions we had to deal with questions that could be easily answered with yes or no. As we became more familiar with the nature of the sources, they became more vocal. Yet the energies were always apparent in some manifestation or other.

When my daughter Gabrielle came for a visit at my request while she was hosting the Archangels in her home, specifically so she could do a session during that hosting, I could only hope Gabriel would appear. Elsewhere I touch on the connection Leah recognized during a Gabriel session in the fact that my daughter wore the female version of his name. Still, there is no way to anticipate how the energies will manifest outwardly in a session.

Board Notes, 4-27-11 (with Gabriel, and Gabrielle at the board with Leah)

Q. Well see, I usually take Maybe [his answer to a previous question] to be different. You're not playing with me are you Gabriel? (laughing). You seem a little more... I don't know if this is the right word, but you seem a little more serious tonight. Is that right?
A. ? (more laughing from me)

Q. OK. You know the energy that I'm picking up on around your presence here tonight. Is that my energy?
A. No

Q. But I am picking up on some other level of energy than I'm normally used to in our exchanges.
A. It's not you at the board.

Q. Thank you for that clarification because it makes a lot of sense. You and WF the other night seemed to be a little more vociferous than when I'm on the board. Is that the energy that's

operating?
A. Maybe

Here Gabriel is making exactly the point I was trying to describe in other circumstances. The disk had been moving very slowly, and Gabrielle is a much more laid-back person in comparison to me and my energy. My feeling had been that he was being more serious, and it was only when I pushed the question of my perception that he volunteered that it wasn't me (my energy) at the board.

In the last of those questions, my reference to his being more vociferous the other night was when Elise was on the board with Leah, mother and daughter; another energy configuration, but this wasn't the time to pursue that.

There's another point here also, and that lies in what kinds of answers I can get to questions about others, even my own children, when they're not present.

Q. And I would like to know...and I'm asking these questions as much for her as I am for myself, because you know how my mind works, but we'll just assume all that... Does her vocabulary, her voracious appetite for the written word and command of the language have something to do with the job that she is here to do?
A. Yes

Q. I don't know if it was you or WF that I asked that question to, and I probably didn't ask it the same way, because I didn't get the answer that I expected, and the answers have more clarity tonight because Gabrielle is here?
A. Yes

I think I should probably say right here that if I'm asking about someone who is not present, and I might be violating their privacy, I will ask if it's appropriate to pursue a line of questioning. But I don't want to create the impression that I will encroach where privacy is an issue. Caution rules.

And a little example of Gabriel's humor surfaces right here as well.

Q. The job that she is here to do, is she more aware of it than she realizes just below the level of her consciousness?
A. No

Q. Are you saying she has no idea?
A. She doesn't want to know.

Q. (L) Does it have anything to do with the baby?
A. Yes

(L) I totally understand that
Q. OK. He's not going to grow up to be a baseball player!
A. You want to know too much.

(I'm already rolling around laughing before he even finishes) Now this is the Gabriel I know. You and WF must be hanging around a lot together.
Q. And I've been told that I know too much!
A. Yes

A major breakthrough in energetic influences came with a visit from one of my closest friends who I hadn't seen in years, though we e-mail regularly, and talk occasionally. Our relationship has a very strong intellectual component, and the time he was here, as Leah observed, we never shut up. I had asked WF for some feedback on the possibility of my friend, JP, taking to the idea of the board, and he advised caution.

The energy JP brought to the board was not strictly of the intellectual variety, but we are like-minded in a much larger sense. I met him when Gabrielle attended kindergarten, and his wife was her first teacher. I became a room father, and very friendly with her. She continuously remarked that I had to meet her husband, knowing that we would hit it off immediately. We finally met at a YMCA parent event to construct a large jungle gym project, and the rest was history.

I was immediately gifted with a trove of books JP had already read, and that continued to be his habit. I considered him to be one of the more influential people to come into my life, as others had, to raise my understanding in one way or another, and JP took it to another whole level. I hadn't been much into the UFO issues beyond a passing curiosity, and his influence extended beyond the mere surface issue, into the deeper areas of technology and other conceptual material. He eventually became a certified MUFON investigator, and probably the only person with whom I could discuss the more far-out subjects that interested me.

So I broached the board subject carefully by segueing through some sociopolitical issues, spicing them with my usual brand of heightened spiritual perspective, then dropped the bomb. No problem. He went right for it, and before I knew it, he was working out the evening schedule to ensure that we'd get a session in before bed, and maybe another next day, before he had to leave.

We did. Both. And if Elise brought WF to the board, JP brought WF's voice. Up until that time we had never had so many answers that were full sentences. Eventually, near the end of the session, after a particularly long answer, I had to inquire of WF what that was about, and what do you suppose he had to say about it?

Board Notes, 5-10-11, joined by JP, Luciano and Leah at the board.

Q. So can you answer that or should we restate it?
A. Yes. Truth is truth. It has no boundary or scope. It is. Truth knows no boundaries.

Lots of jumping in for all as WF just kept going when we thought he had finished several times. And a big WOW for all at the end.

(V) (to JP) I can't wait to transcribe this, because this is the most... OK
Q. Is your prolific use of the language a result of the intellectual energy here tonight?
A. Yes

Q. Is this something like, that you guys arranged on some level?
A. No. It's energy.

Q. So this is like the way charges interact?
A. Yes

Q. So we made it happen?
A. Yes. It is you.

Q. So we should do this more often?
A. Yes. Like minds

I explain to JP that I've always expressed a desire for that

Q. So there's really a lot of energy there!
A. Yes

Q. Well, I don't have to tell you. You know how profound it is!
A. Yes

So there it was straight from the horse's mouth. The energy interaction with my good friend JP, and our level of intellectual discourse, produced the most prolific answers I had ever gotten from the source. And this is one of those sessions that created so much work for me in transcribing because we had gotten into so many in-depth discussions on just about every subject we covered. In transcribing the session I had to redact so much because there were just paragraphs and paragraphs of discussion.

I think some of the questions and answers deserve some sampling here just to make the point that it wasn't limited to just JP and me; Leah was included as well. I was asking about one of the feral cats we feed, who is old and not well at all. I had only wanted to know if she was dying, and if I could do anything for her.

Board Notes, continued:

Q. I just want to ask real fast about the cats. Ma Kitty. Is she dying?
A. Everything dies to themselves.

(L) Does that even make grammatical sense? (V) Yes, everything dies to themselves, because infinite consciousness is everywhere. The fucking rock knows it's a rock and it knows it's gonna die because someone is gonna come along and pulverize it. And eventually some part of the rock, because it got pulverized, will be taken up by a creature as part of its food, and will be absorbed into that creature's life consciousness... (L) And eventually will wind up being shit...(some laughing around) (V) No No No. What I'm saying is that it's entering different levels of consciousness. You know, one of the pathways through the infinite levels of consciousness. And of course, since we're already anywhere that we could have been in infinity, it's just a matter of moving our awareness to have the experience. Now, I want to move on to the cats thing!

Q. Is there anything I could do for her in her condition?
A. She had a life.
Thank you

Q. (L) Does that mean...this is terrible, this is a question a sixty year old will ask: I got a little glimpse at that kind of thing, she had a life, and I started thinking I had a life, and that it's done. Is that what you're talking about when you said mommy cat had a life?
A. You need to understand that you are special and you shouldn't think that way.

(V) OK, I'm going to think of that as current, but I'm going to pursue that... (L) Mommy Cat? (V) No, your little thing there, and once I have it transcribed I'll remember. I'm also going to pursue that state of mind that Leah was expressing, because that really surprised me.

That statement from WF to Leah was by far the longest single answer we had ever received to any question for ourselves, and right up there with the previous example I gave to the question I'd posed for JP regarding truth. And since that session, the answers became much more lengthy and insightful, the source seeming to have become that much more vociferous. It will be seen throughout these chapters as an undercurrent how personalities contribute their energies, which in turn are picked up by the source and incorporated into the output.

I had been living with Leah for some months when a minor conflict I had with her landlord developed into a major crisis for her, and I left. I had some work to do for my sister, and stayed there for a couple of weeks, then returned to my brother's house, where I had spent the entire previous year before going to Leah's house. When she brought my things, she also brought the board. We did a session, and she left the board with me. How peculiar, that I was now looking at the possibility of having Marie, the woman I'd first considered as a board partner prior to ever creating it, to step in and bring her own energy to the project. She was more than willing, and I knew it was only going to be a matter of acclimating her to the process and principles of operation.

And I would be lax in failing to mention that the circle of influence works in both directions: the attendees are at least equally, if not more, influenced by their participation. JP's question and answer sessions provided him a lot of insight into his active role in the local politics of his home state, where he had been spinning his wheels in one sense, but working towards propagating certain truths in another.

Not only was JP profusely thankful, but when I sent him the transcripts of his sessions, he asked me for copies of the session tapes so he could tap in to all the dialogue that never makes it into the transcripts, where we frequently discuss issues that lead to the construction of the actual questions we ask. There is also the factor of the energetic levels of the whole atmosphere so apparent in the audio.

Nor can I exclude all the valuable insight my daughter and I received about familial issues for which I could only get limited information until she attended, bringing not only her own energy, but also the permission of her personal interest, without which I would have been intruding into her privacy. What we discovered about her own son was literally mind-blowing, including by extension the same kind of information about my son, her brother. This rings true also for Leah's daughter, who got insight into her vocational direction, as well as other-life karmic issues she has to resolve with people who are now influencing the the path of her current lifetime.

When we were told by WF that the energy evolving through the board was about like minds, he could not have been more correct. Not only did Leah, Elise and I share other lives, but so Gabriel and I also. In the course of our first session with JP I knew what the answer was going to be when I asked about other lives we shared, because I had already seen them on my own. We were together in three very major life experiences, the nature of which involved many of the kinds of evolutionary changes humanity is facing today, and it just so happened that those lifetimes also were shared with Leah. That would explain how they just connected on the occasion of their first meeting, on JP's visit.

Yes, there is a circle of influence, and it continues to manifest as we continue to discreetly expand the attendees who we think will be compatible with our own energies, and who can put aside their cherished beliefs long enough to expand their horizons, as well as ours. It is an ever expanding circle; a universe unto itself.

Dearly Departed (and Others)

The most commonly disputed idea about the death of the physical body is probably the question of whether or not consciousness survives. From there it raises the next series of questions as to where that consciousness resides, whether it retains memory, and if it reincarnates.

As I said in the Introduction, the first entity to appear on the board for our first, short-lived, session, was my closest friend from early adulthood. It seemed strange after-the-fact that we closed the session immediately that we bade him farewell, because my state of mind in having been so caught by surprise left me totally unprepared to engage him in my usual style of banter.

That was the very last time in any board session that I was so indisposed, even when facing some of the nastier visitors we had occasion to encounter. My disappointment in letting that opportunity to chat with Alan pass was almost immediate, when I finally gained some perspective. So when others, familiar and stranger, came to visit, always at the beginning of a session, I simply remained centered in my usual demeanor, and let things develop, or not, as any given situation dictated.

Any number of discarnates (literally, *not* flesh), as I've taken to identifying them, showed up on our board, so it became rather routine. In that class I put not only those we may have known in our lifetimes, but also those we seem never to have known, and those who seem never to have incarnated into physical realities.

To me this begs the question that has plagued mankind over the many millennia of our histories, and likely just as well in prehistory: just what is the nature of these realities (I use the plural as a matter of preference) in all the many forms it likely takes?

Here comes another can of worms, and I admit that this chapter was intended to explore the infinite possibilities of infinite lifeforms in infinite universes with infinite dimensions. It was the Law of One series, said to have been issued from another density of reality through its spokesperson/complex (?) Ra, that gave the twentieth century its first inkling of the more complex nature of reality in an alternative to academic science and structured religious thought and belief.

Ra, as I've already said in a previous chapter, was channeled by a dedicated Christian woman named Carla Rueckert, who was put into trance by her mentor and life-companion Don Elkins, and in the company of a confidant named James McCarthy, who recorded and transcribed the sessions over the many years they engaged the project.

It is from those session that we are given the tremendous insight into the true nature of the universe and our places in it. For starters, it is the first place where I personally came upon the concept of densities, which explains the hierarchy, if you will, of the manifestations of The One in all forms of matter, sentient and not.

The term is frequently used interchangeably with the term dimensions, but in fact it could be said that they are each aspects of the other, and an understanding of that relationship is necessary to the appreciation of the challenges that arise in any communication with those who have "passed over".

I will make this explanation as short and sweet as possible in order to dispense with the technicalities as expeditiously as possible, yet sufficiently to resolve any confusion as to the intermingling of these aspects of reality. Humans, as we know ourselves to be, generally reside in the third density, yet many in today's parlance insist we are in the third dimension. We know however that we perceive three dimensions of space - length, width and height, and one dimension of time -now. It follows that our third density is therefor four dimensional.

The Law of One gives us to understand that fourth density will find us comprehending those same spatial dimensions, with the addition of three dimensions of time - past, present and future. This is a difficult concept for many people to accept, but I have related elsewhere, in the chapter on other lives, that reincarnation is merely a linear way of attempting to understand the more complex soul-level experience of multiple lifetimes occurring at once, with a present-time focus of the human consciousness in the here and now.

And at last we come to the point where I can say that it is exactly this problem that we are always facing when communicating with those who are no longer in this limited third density focus.

It is generally understood by many in the alternative spiritual community (sorry, no other convenient labeling choices) that those who have left this density will usually find themselves in fifth density. Where third density is to be considered the lowest of the conscious awareness densities, being primarily a physical density, fourth is considered to be less physical and more spiritual, though the latter term hardly implies 'good'. Spiritual in this context means having less physical attributed, and more ethereal attributes.

Going up the chain to fifth, at least for those whose residence there commences with their departure from third density in the context of this discussion, we would be encountering a completely ethereal environment, yet accompanied by the baggage accumulated in the time spent in what we call this lifetime.

It seems the challenge for those residents is their inability to distinguish events which they may be observing in our here-and-now, or in our future, as having the time relevance that it does for us. Then there is the additional issue of alternative realities that they are observing, but which are only on the horizon as possibilities that have yet to be actualized.

So an observer who has passed to that density may see someone in this density dying, and perceive it as being imminent, when in fact it may be years of our time from actually happening. They may have concerns about their own observations of another's lifetime in our density based solely on the judgments they would have made had they still been here observing in real time.

Caution is always advised in any interpretation of what may be received from that realm when it is not otherwise immediately obvious in its accuracy. There are many stories people tell about sessions with psychics where they have received both very accurate and extremely inaccurate information, and everything in between.

I can relate such an experience I personally had at a psychic session about which I subsequently inquired at the board, and the whole thing was really quite humorous, both during and after. Leah had arranged for us to attend a session with about forty people total. I had met the psychic, Scot, at a Christmas cocktail party he hosted for his patrons.

He was quite down to earth and sincere, and I knew his abilities to have been among the more highly developed. What I liked most about him was that he would just jump right into character as the person who was coming through, and that helped tremendously in relating to a relationship with the entity. This was not your run of the mill "I'm getting someone with a J" kind of deal. This was the real thing, no guessing.

As Leah and I were dressing to go, I chose a pair of Dockers that I hadn't worn in at least a year, and when I buttoned the waist I was concerned it would pop, so I wore a belt and left the button undone, leaving my shirt un-tucked. I was still somewhat uncomfortable. On the way there I told Leah I was going to remain skeptical, even if it seemed I had someone coming through for me. We mingled downstairs at the restaurant that was closed for the season, and by the time we went up to the large room where the session was being held, most of the seats were taken, but there were two seats together down in the front on one side, and Leah directed us there.

Scot meditated silently for a few minutes, then looked around the room, and got in character. He acted out a person who said his name was Joe, and that he was a very simple man, who didn't brag and didn't like braggarts. He had played the harmonica and the violin, though not professionally. I looked at Leah. This was my father, but I wasn't saying anything. He went on with a few more things, like they didn't have anyone where he was who had hair like mine, and she kept nudging me to speak up, but I hesitated. Then it came. "And I know your pants are too tight, and you're worried you're gonna pop a button", and we both lost it.

In the exchange that followed, he said I needed to pay more attention to my health, and a few other fatherly things. I tried to keep it less intimate with forty people in the room, but in the end I was still quite moved. After the session we went downstairs to the restaurant and had snacks and beverages, and we mingled more intimately. I really had a great time talking with people about their experiences at the session, and of course I got a lot of comments about my tight pants, even to the point of lifting my shirt for someone who insisted on seeing the proof.

One more point, is that we had only parted company with the Arch Angels a few days before this, and I was still very fond of invoking them and the Magdalene in many places I went, so I had summoned them at this session with Scot, and prior to beginning the session he commented that the energy in the room was really powerful. Leah had been picking it up, and mentioned it to me.

Board Notes, 5-15-11.

Q. Was I seeing the Magdalene's smiling face for real?
A. Yes (the disk flew to Yes before I was done the question)
[This was a reference to a meditation a few days prior]

Q. Were the angels... I meditated last night [at the Scot session). Did we have the angels and the Magdalene in the room

last night?
A. Yes

Q. Is that the energy that Scot was exclaiming about?
A. Yes

Q. (L) Is that the energy that I felt on the right side of my body?
A. Yes
(I was seriously chuckling at the thought of that, like who knew)
(L) How come I felt it on the right side of my body?
(V) Because that's where I was! (laughing)

Q. Did her feeling that on the right side of her body have anything to do with my being on her right side?
A. Maybe
That means we could explore that!

Q. That really was my father coming through last night!
A. Yes

Q. Now I'm surprised, because I really would have expected him to take advantage of the opportunity to come through in this format. Was that energy last night just more conducive to his...
A. Yes

Q. So did I really get everything that he intended to communicate last night, or does that still have to sink in? I got it?
A. No

Q. Was it because of the circumstances?
A. You didn't want to hear it. (we both began spelling it out loud ahead of the letters)

Q. But I knew that didn't I?
A. Yes
(L) You didn't want to hear it!

Q. And what I didn't want to hear was about (L) Your health... (V) My health.
A. Yes

Q. And is that because he was seeing something that I'm already aware of?
A. No

Q. Oh, he was seeing something that I'm not aware of!
A. He is seeing his role as your father.

Q. So he was just doing what father's do!
A. Yes

Q. Because that just brings up another question: was that just based on his own... and I'm just going to call it baggage, not in any derogatory sense, was that based on his own baggage that he brought there because you bring that stuff to fifth density after you move on?
A. Yes

Q. And so a lot of those entities that were coming through were coming through with their own baggage!
A. Yes

Q. And people don't understand that when they're hearing it!
A. Right
(L) Can we have a discussion and pause the tape? (V) Yes. Let me just ask one more quickie.

Q. Does Scot understand that?
A. Yes
(We pause for a discussion relative to the 5D baggage thing and Scot's frequent references to it that Leah has been aware of in other sessions with him)

Q. So whatever my father was trying to communicate to me in

his role as my father, and with his baggage, was there something in that message beyond that, that I needed to get, that I didn't get?
A. Only that he loves you.

Q. Only that he loves me, which he was never able to say in his physical sojourn!
A. Right (we always chuckle when WF uses that idiom)

Q. (L) But he wouldn't come to try to communicate if he didn't!
A. Right (so we chuckle even harder)
(V) We have to get that on the board!

That was one reference to the baggage, but there are more. And this is as true in board sessions as it is in the kind of psychic session we were attending with Scot. I can't emphasize enough how crucial it is to keep that in mind, not just for the information you might get, but also for the information you might be requesting. Sometimes we might be suggesting an answer without realizing it, and the answer might be projected to us from the perspective of the board guest's more expansive view of time, and also particular alternative realities. Here are two interesting examples. The first is Leah's father, from a very early session also attended by Leah's daughter.

Board Notes, 1-26-11 [Early transcript answers were all caps, and I left it that way here]

Q. Hello?
A. GOODBYE HELLO

Q. Is this our sixth density source?
A. NO

Q. Who is this?
A. WALT

Q. (L) Dad is this you?
A. YES

Q. (L) Hi pop!
A. HELLO

Q. (L) Why are you coming through? Do you have something to communicate?
A. YES

Q. (L) About mom?
A. YES

Q. (L) What can you tell us about mom?
A. SICK

Q. (L) Is there something we can do?
A. NO

Q. (L) Is this what she wants?
A. YES

Q. (L) Are you just telling us to be aware?
A. YES

Q. (L) Is she going to move?
A. NO

Q. (L) Is she going to die soon?
A. MAYBE

Q. (L) What was the source of the info I got when I was thinking about that?
A. ME

Q. (L) Is there anything I can do?
A. NO

Q. (L) If its "maybe" is she committed to this?
A. MAYBE

Q. (L) Is this going to be sudden?
A. YES

Q. (L) Is this something to tell my brothers?
A. NO

Q. (L) can she see you now?
A. YES

Q. (L) Is this just a heads up - no seriously?
A. YES

Q. (L) Anything else to know?
A. NO

Q. (L) Is that why you came here?
A. YES

Q. (L) Is anyone else there waiting to talk to us?
A. YES

Q. (L) With you now?
A. YES

Q. (L) Who is with you right now?
A. PHIL

Q. (L) Is it Phil?
A. YES

Q. (L) Is this someone we know?
A. NO

Q. (L) Someone who has something to communicate?

A. YES

Q. (L) Does Elise know him?
A. TOMORROW

Q. (L) Is there anything else dad?
A. NO

Q. (L) Say goodbye dad.
A. GOODBYE

As it happened, Leah's mother had not been well over the prior few years, the particulars of her condition being irrelevant. But the fact is, she didn't die, and she did move almost two years later, after repeated incidents of having needed someone in the home more akin to what we know as an assisted living arrangement. This also points up one of the difficulties in asking what may seem to be leading questions for the convenience of expediting the communication.

The proof of that last sticky point came when a very close friend and former band-member of Leah's son died suddenly of an accidental overdose only a few days before. Was it accidental? Seems so! But what we're after here is how we may be projecting into the answers we're receiving. And I should say that where it seems appropriate, I include the entire exchange in these departed soul exchanges.

Board Notes, 5-8-11

Q. Hello?
A. Hello

Q. And who do we have with us this evening?
A. Mike

Q. (L) Mike?
A. Yes

Evolving The Spirit Board

Leah explains this is Seth's friend who just died
Q. (V) Is that who this is?
A. Yes

Q. (V) Are you in a good place?
A. Yes

Q. (L) I'm really glad about that, because I'm really sad about what happened. And a lot of people are sad, especially Seth. (V) But you know that right?
A. Yes

Q. (V) Was this something that you intended to do?
A. No

Q. (V) So it was an accident!
A. Yes

Q. (V) But you're accepting of it!
A. Yes

Q. (L) You are in a good place?
A. Yes

He seemed to be having difficulty moving the disk, navigating, as it were.
Q. (V) Is you energy low?
A. No

(L) It's because he doesn't know how to do this.
Q. (V) Do you feel comfortable in manipulating the board from where you are?
A. Not yet

We give him some instruction on how to better maneuver.
Q. (V) Can you see the board from where you are?
A. Yes

Luciano da Uno

Q. (V) Is there something you wanted to impart?
A. Yes

Q. (V) OK. Go ahead.
A. Tell them I'm sorry

Q. (V) You're sorry for the pain they're having?
A. Yes

Q. (L) You were so young, and so talented. Do you know that right now? Do you know what I wrote today on your obituary page?
A. Yes

Q. (L) You know I believe that, that your energy is like a star that's shining on us. And I always loved your energy, especially when you played the drums. You were awesome. You were really really awesome, and you always were, even when you were a little kid. Because you were always a little kid when you played. And to have that talent and have such a short life was unfortunate. But I suppose it was your time. (V) Well, that's what I was going to ask. Is this something that, now that you are there, that it was destined to happen?
A. Yes

Q. (V) So it wasn't just fate!
A. No

Q. (V) And again, from where you are, you're accepting of it and it's OK!
A. Yes

Q. (V) But you feel for the people that you left behind!
A. Yes

Q. (V) Are there others there whom you've known?
A. Not really.

Q. (V) But you are with others!
A. Yes

Q. (V) You do know that there are others that you've known on that side!
A. Yes

Q. (V) And you know that eventually you can hook up with them if that's your desire!
A. Yes

Q. (V) Are you now with entities that will help you acclimate to being there?
A. Yes

Q. (V) So you're just going through the process and you know that!
A. Yes

Q. (L) But you are loved there!
A. Yes

Q. (L) You feel loved!
A. Yes

Q. (V) So, you know, the problem that we always see right away, when others come onto the board and ask us to communicate to them, is how... you know what a delicate subject it is to say 'oh yeah, he came through on the board', you understand that right?
A. Yes

Q. (V) So now, for those people who knew you, in the most personal way, is there something that you could say that we could pass on, that we would know without question that it was absolutely coming from you?
A. Maybe

Q. (V) OK then, give it a shot!
A. Go know

Q. (L) Go know?
A. Yes

Q. (V) Would Seth know that?
A. Yes

Q. (V) Is that something you've said to him?
A. Yes

Q. (V) And obviously we don't know that. Is it more personal?
A. Yes

Q. (V) We definitely will pass that on to Seth. Will that make you content?
A. Yes

Q. (V) Is there anything else you'd like to say?
A. No

Q. (V) We wish you the best in Spirit, because where you are, that is what you'll have. (L) Thank you for communicating with us. (V) We are happy to have you.
A. Good Bye

(V) Well, that was a surprise! And you kind of had the feeling that he was going to stop in.

We Take a Break

Here is a familiar situation where we are faced with having to forward a message from one of these departed souls to family or friends and somehow verify that the board session is a legitimate medium. In this case Leah requested some kind of statement that would serve that purpose for her son. So how did that all pan out?

Board Notes, 5-10-11, with friend JP.

Leah is explaining here at length about her experience when Mike was coming through last night, and the question that arose around our different memory of whether it was 'know go' or 'go know'. She was questioning if some other energy was at work in that whole transaction. And then Seth had no idea as to what that meant, and Leah had to question whether she herself was influencing it.
Q. So what was going on there?
A. The part of you that is not you.

Q. Is this like the duality, the other self, the darker side?
A. No

Q. (L) It's about the ego versus the spiritual self!
A. Maybe

I tell John that this is where you're really working. 'Maybe' usually means it's up to you. You're making a statement that's a question, and then it gets thrown back to you. Now there's another way of it getting thrown back to you, but the 'maybe' is usually an indicator of whether you want it to be or not. If you get a question mark, it's about 'ask yourself'. (L) Come up with the real question. (V) Ask yourself, or come up with the real answer.

Q. Was this an instance that exemplifies the frequency insofar as this is all engrained in her program, or is it more of an aberration? (L) Is it my program?
A. No

Q. So it's more of an aberration?
A. (long circling) No

Q. So does it have something to do with outside sources of energy interacting with her or acting on her, either of those?
A. (more long circling) No

OK. This means something, that he's going so slow.
Q. We're just going in the wrong direction!
A. (long circling) No
We all three laugh our asses off, and John starts to get an idea of how funny WF can really be.

Q. So it's not an aberration, and it's not something external... (L) Can you eat it (we start laughing hard, all three). Is it bigger than a bread box? (more hard laughing) (V) Is it this big? (gesturing) (JP) Is it behind door number two? (more laughing) We calm down.

(V) I'm lost here. So what was happening. (to Leah) Well, it was your ego... (L) So what happened was I said to Seth, 'did Mike ever say go know', and Seth said 'let me think....No.' So it wasn't his thing. And when I said it, the logical part of my brain said 'that's you. That's something you would say. That's not Mike'. In short, Leah was realizing that she somehow got her own head in the answer.

Q. So this was just the ego energy creeping in on its own, to the board , and....
A. (the disk just started going in big strong circles, before I finished the statement, and just shot around to) Yes
We were all amazed at the energy, like the wind up for the pitch. Everyone was remarking something or other. Discussion about who's really doing this. I tell Leah that if we put her into a trance, because she's the channel, she would just start talking and answer every question I put to her. This turns into a real tape-burner.
The bottom line becomes that Spirit is welcome to appear on the board in its highest positive forms, and if you can get here, you're welcome here, just please know how to spell. LOL

Q. So is this about her having more awareness of her ego as it rears its ugly head?
A. Yes

Q. And that's the lesson. So...
A. U R so beautiful
This causes chuckles, because I know WF saw me anticipating the 'you are beautiful' line, and threw me off by injecting so to distract me, and throw some fun into the mix.

Q. (L) Thank you WF!
A. U R Welcome

That should be informative. And certainly this is not the first time this happened. In the Toolbox chapter I relate an incident where Leah was actually given an answer that she wanted herself when she inquired about the timing of the sale of her landlady's house.

These kinds of incidents may throw suspicion over the whole nature of the medium itself, but I would have to suggest that one needs to maintain a certain awareness of one's intent when formulating questions. Speaking for myself, it is always more important to *know*, as opposed to being merely *assured*,

Then there are the occasions where we are asked to make contact with a living relative and it actually works out, and even works out great. For some reason, and I really should inquire about this, almost all of these contacts are Leah's acquaintances. This particular relative returned several times, until we finally delivered on our stated intent to follow through on his request.

Once again though, it is apparent that what is being seen from the perspective of fifth density with respect to time or alternative realities is not how it all shakes out. When it comes to seeing the death of those who are left behind among the living, it is certain that everyone of them is going to die at some point, and I can only imagine that the ability to have the focus option of witnessing a death becomes an overwhelming obsession. Remember, the baggage remains.

Board Notes, 2-15-11

Q. Hello?
A. Hello

Q. Who do we have with us?
A. Barry

Q. (L) Uncle Barry?
A. Yes

Leah exclaims how she'd been thinking of him, and how funny he was
Q. Because I was thinking of you?
A. Yes

Leah recites a litany of her experiences with Uncle Barry, and what she'd been thinking of him
Q. Is that why you're coming through?
A. Yes

Q. What do you want?
A. Tell Val hi

Q. Tell her it came through the board?
A. Yes

We discuss how she would react to being told her father came through a spirit board.
Q. Do you really think she'd go for that?
A. No

Q. What could I tell her that she'd definitely know it came from you?
A. Giver her a rock

We bid Barry goodbye, and ask:
Q. Can we have WF?
A. Yes

Q. Hello?
A. Hello

Q. What's that about with people coming through so frequently at the beginning of a session?
A. They need to.

So here we are being asked to give someone a rock as a sign that we've had a viable communication, and nothing said about its significance to the receiver. I can't say for sure how we were actually taking this particular contact, but apparently it led Leah to inquire as to the status of Barry's daughter.

Board Notes, 3-2-11

Q. Hello?
A. Hello

Q. Is this WF?
A. Maybe

Q. OK, who do we have?
A. Barry

Q. (L) Is this Uncle Barry
A. Yes.

I didn't send the rock

Q. What is it you have to say?
A. Give Val the rock

Q. Is that because she needs the rock?

A. Yes

Q. Is that because you need to give to her?
A. No.

Q. You just want to give it to her?
A. Yes.

Q. She will know that this is from you then, right?
A. Yes.

Q. It doesn't have to be a big rock, does it?
A. Yes.

Q. It does have to be a big rock?
A. Yes

Q. See, because I was going to mail it. Will she be afraid, will it make her more paranoid? You know Val is paranoid, right?
A. Yes

Q. Is that all you wanted Uncle Barry, to tell me to do that rock thing?
A. Yes

Q. OK, we'll find a way to do it. Can you let WF come through now?
A. Yes.

Thank you.

Another first for us: A departed contact, and family at that, who comes through to follow up on a request. And Barry wasn't done.

Board Notes, 3-17-11, 3:30 ish

Q. Hello?
A. Hello

Q. And who do we have?
A. Barry

Q. (L)I kinda thought you were going to show up at some point. I talked to my mother today and we don't know what's going on. Val won't call us back. Is that why you showed up before, there's something wrong with Tracy?
A. Yes

Q. Is there anything I can do without hearing from her?
A. Go see her.

Q. Go see her?
A. Yes

Q. (V) that is in the plan somewhere. Is Leah seeing her somehow going to produce beneficial energy in the outcome of the circumstances?
A. Yes

Q. (V)Are you seeing what Tracy's problem is? Is there something you can contribute in terms of information that would help her, or help us help her?
A. No

Q. (L)So your help is mostly for Val? (V)Support?
A. Yes

Q. Is it enough that you know we're working on it right now?
A. Maybe

Q. Well, do you see anything more, that we could do more immediately?
A. Maybe

Q. If you think there's something that you want to recommend, you should say it now while you have the opportunity.
A. Go see her.

Q. We will ask WF about that. Is that OK?
A. Yes

Q. Do you know about our relationship with WF?
A. Yes.

Q. (L) Is he there now
A. Yes

Q. (L)Can we speak to him?
A. Yes

Now that is persistence! And isn't it odd that with all the perspective one has in that realm, there is no information available that would help the loved ones here on the Earth plane. But this wasn't over yet anyhow, and the death issue finally emerges.

Board Notes, 3-18-11

Q. Hello?
A. Hello

Q. Who do we have?
A. Barry

Q. (L)Hello Uncle Barry. I talked to my mother today and Tracy is out of the hospital. They brought her home. Val brought her home, and she still needs our prayers, but she's home. And my mother told her that I wanted to see her, and it is being arranged. Is that OK?
A. Yes

Q. (L) Can we have WF now?
A. No

Q. (V) What else do you need Barry?
A. Tracy is going to die.

Q. (L) And you're worried about Val?
A. Yes

Q. (L) I'm worried about Val too. Tracy has been her entire life for as old as Val is, and I'm worried about Val too. (V) Let me ask you something. From where you are is it possible that you could send Val a sign so she'll know that when Tracy passes over she'll be fine?
A. You are supposed to do that.

Q. (V) Yes, we know that, But I'm talking about reinforcing it until she gets your message from us. And if that's not possible I understand. I know that even this is not easy for you. (L) We know that you were brave in order to come through and do this. (V) So do you think it will be enough just our giving her that message?
A. Yes

Q. (V) And we can tell her that you are in a good place and that Tracy will be joining you?
A. Yes

We discuss scheduling that with Val
Q. Will that be soon enough?
A. Maybe

Q. (L)You don't know about time there, right?
A. (Inaudible, but I think it was No)

Q. (V)Is that OK?
A. Yes

Q. (V)I'm sure that whatever support you can give from where you are, you and other loved ones, you are giving it.
A. Yes

Q. (V)So we're all doing what we can and trying to accept the inevitability of our mortality. So Can we have WF now?
A. Yes

Q. WF?
A. Yes

Q. So, did we handle that well?
A. Maybe

Q. Time will tell?
A. Yes

Q. Does he realize that we're doing what we can do when we can do it?
A. No

Q. Is the perspective so different where he is that the fetters of our corporeal reality are easy for him to miss?
A. Yes

Q. Eventually he will understand?
A. Yes

I thought it relevant to get our exchange with WF after the contact, because Barry doesn't understand that we're doing what we can, and it's all a matter of perspective, in spite of the seemingly superior access one has to other types of information in that density. We were intending to make the trip to see Val, but couldn't get it together. We mentioned it to WF.

Board Notes, 3-23-11

Q. We were going to try to go see Tracy today, and that doesn't look like it's happening. Does Val know that Tracy is dying?
A. No

Q. Does Tracy know that she's dying?
A. Yes

Q. Is she putting on the courageous face for her mother?
A. Always

Q. Does Barry see that from his vantage point?
A. Yes

And once again, what becomes Barry's final demonstration of persistence, but this time to convey his gratitude.

Board Notes 3-29-11

Q. Hello?
A. Hello

Q. And who do we have?
A. Barry

Q. I felt you around. Did you feel that I felt you around?
A. Yes

Q. Are you pleased with our effort?
A. Yes

Q. Do you think that it had a positive effect?
A. Yes

Q. Did you see me bonding with Tracy?
A. Yes

Q. Was that good for her?

A. Yes

(L) she's a sweetie
(V) She is a sweetie, I'm telling you, she and I bonded when we were leaving. She and I really bonded.

Q. OK, let's talk about the rock, because Val was totally confused (L) but moved (V) but moved, it was a moving experience (L)Scary for me (V) So can you tell us what the rock meant for you that she was gifted with it?
A. she needed to see the strength in herself

(L) So she was right that you called her the rock, right?
A. Yes

Q. Was she buying the explanation that you were coming to Leah in meditation?
A. Yes

Q. Can we pass that on that she needed to see the strength in herself?
A. Yes

Q. (L)So we can tell her that right?
A. Yes

Q. So are you happy?
A. Yes
(L)You know she said that she's open to you visiting her and communicating with her. I communicate with my dad. I know when my dad is coming to me. I get some kind of sign and I know that it's him.

Q. So the bottom line is could you reach her?
A. Yes

Q. Was this an opening for you to be able to have access to her?

A. Yes

Q. let me just make a remark here: it's great to have somebody with a facility for the board that you do, because, I'll tell you what, you really know how to spell. Laughing (L)and I don't, so this is all you. (V) No, I mean it's great the way you use the board. Are you aware of that?
A. Yes

Q. Is there anything else that you'd like to comment on, contribute, say?
A. Just thanks.

Q. You're welcome, and thank you, because it was a very meaningful experience for us as well. (L)me too. It was a breakthrough experience. I lost the spit in my mouth, so I do know. (we are both laughing a lot at this point) So thank you.
A. Good bye

Q. Good bye.
(V) Yeah, that was a very positive experience. I really did feel him around. (L) I wanted to talk to you about it. (we went to pause to talk about it, and what a moving experience it was to talk to Val and Tracy)
(V)And I don't know what's appropriate at this point. (L) We need to talk to WF (V) or whatever positive forces are there.

I can hardly convey what a moving experience that was for me, it being my first meeting of Val and Tracy, in a pizza joint. We had been running all day in the city and made that our last stop, just around the dinner hour. I was absolutely taken with Tracy, who being in her twenties had the appearance of young teenage girl. And the bonding experience we had truly touched my soul.

It is a memory that will live with me forever. When I saw them again about eighteen months later, we were right back to that bonding state. And what may have seemed for Barry, from his perspective, to have been the imminent death of his granddaughter, again proved to be unfounded. She was as lively as the first time I saw her, and seemed to be looking forward to her life, however challenging it must be.

Another of Leah's departed uncles was only interested in seeing the larger family remain in touch, and after many years of being on that side, saw the opportunity to make his feelings known. This one really surprised me insofar as his mention of his own grave, and the frequent visits of his survivors. And once again, Leah is being asked to make contact and somehow explain how she's received this information and direction from a deceased relative. The special twist in this one is that the surviving son is now a minister.

Board Notes, 5-3-11

Q. Hello
A. Hello

Q. And who do we have with us this evening?
A. George

Q. OK George. Have you joined us before?
A. No

Q. Does one of us know you?
A. Yes

Q. Which one of us would that be?
A. Leah

Q. (L) Is this Uncle George?
A. Yes

Q. (L) High Uncle George. My father's brother. You know, sometimes I think about you, because I was young when you died. But I remember the story around it, and you died... you

pulled your car over and died in the car. Did you know that that was happening? Is that why you pulled the car over?
A. Yes

Q. (L)Were you scared?
A. No

Q. (V) Was that because on another level you had accepted where you were going and what it was about?
A. Yes

Q. (L) And was it because Aunt Marge died?
A. unstated, but it must have been No

Q. (L) You just accepted death!
A. Yes

Q. (L) And you were... I'll just put it this way, you were looking forward to being with God!
A. Yes

Q. (V) Are you with Walt?
A. Yes

Q. (V) So I guess then you know that he's been here!
A. Yes

(L) But Uncle George was much more religious. They were church... My cousin George is now a minister.

Q. (V) Were you attracted to the energy here, and you saw that it gave you an opportunity to appear?
A. Yes

Q. (V) And you saw, on whatever level it works there, you saw that Walt had been here and been able to convey what he wanted!

A. Yes

Q (L) And I think you also saw that we are not dabbling in the dark arts, and that we are also coming here with open hearts and open minds, and looking for the highest spiritual entities, correct?
A. Yes

Q. (L) Is there anything that you want to tell us?
A. Yes

Q. (V) OK, go ahead. I hope you can spell!
A. Go to the grave.

Q. (L) Of you.... your grave?
A. Yes

Q. (V) Why do you want her to do that?
A. See the family.

Q. (V) Your family? Your living family?
A. Yes

Q. (V) Do they come there frequently
A. Yes

Q. (V) OK. Why do you want her to see the family?
A. To know them

Q. (L) You're right. I don't have much contact with George or Martha. (V) Do you want her to do that for them?
A. No

Q. (V) For what reason, if you can enunciate it?
A. For family

Q. (V) Because you want to see the family remain integrated!

A. Yes

Q. (V) So should this appear to be.... (to Leah) Are they buried together, near your father? (L) I don't know. Is everyone at Sunset Memorial?
A. Yes

Q. (L) Are you there too?
A. Yes

Q. (L) I'm not sure about that. I don't know. (V) And would you like this to appear as though it's accidental?
A. No

Q. (V) You want her to let them know that you were in contact with her?
A. (no response)

Q. (V) That's a hard one isn't it, because your son's a minister!
A. Yes

Q. (L) That would be really difficult. (V) So then what's your bottom line in how she approaches this. Just get with your feelings about it. OK. I know you're motivated by love, and that it's love of family spirit, is that it?
A. Yes

Q. (V) And... but would it be okay with you if it just appeared to be accidental, an accidental meeting?
A. Yes

Q. (V) So it's not so important that they know that your consciousness survived beyond the physical, an... in other words you don't want to interfere with anyone's belief systems!
A. No

Q. (L) And Uncle George, I know. I think about that, and I

remember the family talking about that. He left for work and pulled over to the side of the road and died. And I've tried to imagine ...(V) Are you concerned for their well-being?
A. No

Q. (V) Where you are, do you see the evolving events that are developing here on the Earth?
A. Yes

Q. (V) And where you are it's easy to accept whatever consequences evolve, even as far as your family is concerned!
A. Yes

Q. (V) Because you see the bigger picture!
A. Yes

Q. (V) Has your spirit reincarnated on the Earth?
A. No

Q. (V) Do you see that happening anytime soon, in our time, the way we see time?
A. No

Q. (V) You have no desire to?
A. No

(L) That was kind of emphatic!
Q. (V) We'll have to ruminate over that. Is that enough for the time being, knowing that you can come back at any time? Like Uncle Barry! (L) But that's a different family. (V) Well that doesn't matter. Do you know Barry where you are?
A. No

Q. So you know you can return anytime to further your cause!
(L) Is Aunt Annie with you?
A. Yes

Q. (L) Will you say Hi to her for me?
A. Yes

Q. I miss my Aunt Annie. I miss her a lot!
A. She knows.

Q. (L) Thank you for making me cry. (V) So, is that enough for this evening?
A. Yes

Q. Well then we bid you adieu, and welcome you to return when you have good cause, and we will be considering your request.
A. Good Bye.

We never did make the trip to the cemetery, so this is one for the future if it is to be. That will be Leah's choice. But I would like to point out how emphatic George's answer was when I asked if he had reincarnated yet, and then if he had any desire to. I won't speculate at this juncture what the fifth density plane must offer in the infinite variety of purposes it must serve, but apparently there are those who are quite comfortable there and have no desire to move on.

And for the sake of contrast, and to save the reader having to search around the book for these examples, and I'm including here those other instances of less friendly or less directed discarnates who made appearances. First is the Hag.

Board Notes, 1-18-11

Q. Hello?
A. Hello

Disk is spiraling and circling

Q. Can we get some indication as to the spiraling and circling?
A. HELL

Q. What?
A. HELL

Q. Who is this source?
A. KKGGJ

Q. Is this a discarnate entity ?
A. IBHAGG

We repeat our invocation of the higher self again

Then there was the very resentful Sam.

Board Notes, 6-13-11

Q. Hello?
A. Hello

Q. And who do we have with us this evening?
A. Sam

Q. Do we know you?
A. No

Q. OK. What can we do for you?
A. Go to hell.

Q. (L) Go to hell? (surprised)
A. Yes

Q. (V) Obviously you're not a very happy spirit!
A. No

Q. So, do you have some grudge that you're holding?
A. Yes

Q. OK. Against whom?

A. The ones that killed me

Q. The ones that killed you!
A. Yes

Q. How long has this been, in our time?
A. I don't know

Q. (L) You seem very articulate on the board. You've done this before? (the disk was flowing quite methodically)
A. Yes

Q. (V) With others?
A. Yes

Q. Has anyone offered to help you resolve your problem?
A. Yes

Q. And do you want to resolve your problem?
A. I try

Q. You try. OK. In the place where you are, have you met anyone to help you resolve it?
A. No

Q. Do you want to meet someone to help you resolve it?
A. Good Bye

For those who will be indulging the Spirit Board experience in sincerity, you should at least expect to have some dearly departed visitors to your sessions. Be prepared for anything, but don't allow yourself to be sucked-in to negative energies. Wish those who are troubled the best, and let them go. For family or close friends and acquaintances, indulge them with the love you had for them when they were here, and decide for yourself how you want to interact, and what you're willing to do. Don't make promises, but if you say you'll try to do something that is requested of you, try to remember that one day you may find yourself on the other side and hoping for an intermediary.

Tapping The Toolbox

The tools available to those of us working in the positive energies are myriad, and we are legion. We may be out in the public eye interacting in Spirit, or in the nursery preparing a new generation of those who will manifest Spirit in its infinite forms as we are navigating the paths that lead to the One place, and that place is awareness.

The levels of experience we access with the conscious mind are augmented only by our desire for exploration at any given point in our ever evolving understanding, and access to the deeper levels of the unconscious are paramount to our integrating our potential. The board is only one of the tools we have available to have that greater access.

We did not come to the board on a whim. As I think I've already said elsewhere, I had been entertaining the idea for some months before I even mentioned it to Leah, and we talked about it for a while before we undertook to design and create it. But it is even more important that I had spent the greater part of my life in spiritual study, guided by Spirit to every next step in the process of honing awareness, and grooming myself energetically, through both positive and seemingly negative experience.

When Leah and I reconnected after many years, we had additional work to do as a unit rekindling the energy of our work as twin flames, and maturing our understanding as travelers in this sojourn.

When we did finally come to the board, which I've covered in the introduction, it was a responsibility we did not take lightly. We didn't just go out and buy a Ouija Board or Spirit Board and then sit down to summon whatever spirits made themselves known to us in whatever haphazard fashion such things may occur. We had already decided that we were going to proceed cautiously, and I invite the reader to make note of those experiences as we have set them out previously.

The board is a tool in the toolbox of consciousness, and if you have not already reconciled yourself to the spiritual guidance that should form the foundation of your endeavors to acquire the kind of knowledge you can receive from any source, whether material or ethereal, I would caution against it. I have heard many stories of dark ethereal entities manifesting on Ouija Boards over the years, and they usually consist of people sorely prepared for any more than a quick thrill of the parlor game variety.

We were in pursuit of the highest energies of the higher self as it may mysteriously dwell in realms that could possibly be made available through such a source as the board. We entertained no naivete in believing we would simply connect to the most positive energies in our first attempt, so we were prepared to encounter any number of improbable connections, and to deal with them in the highest spiritual way we knew.

For those who are interested in safeguarding their efforts on a board, I can only offer the invocation we developed from the time of our first session, through the experiences that allowed us to see its shortcomings, and with the additional help of our guide in these matters as we navigated through the dimensional planes that were accessible through the medium.

We invoke the energy of the combined higher self as a point of contact, in Love, with open hearts and open minds. We invite the highest positive energies of Spirit to manifest here as appropriate to the circumstances.

This proved to be more than adequate once we were guided

to evolving it to the form it now takes, even where we were tested at one point when our normal source contact allowed a resentfully troubled discarnate entity to manifest and express some very negative energy.

Board Notes, 6-13-11

Q. Hello?
A. Hello

Q. And who do we have with us this evening?
A. Sam

Q. Do we know you?
A. No

Q. OK. What can we do for you?
A. Go to hell.

Q. (L) Go to hell? (surprised)
A. Yes

Q. (V) Obviously you're not a very happy spirit!
A. No

Q. So, do you have some grudge that you're holding?
A. Yes

Q. OK. Against whom?
A. The ones that killed me

Q. The ones that killed you!
A. Yes

Q. How long has this been, in our time?
A. I don't know

Q. (L) You seem very articulate on the board. You've done this before? (the disk was flowing quite methodically)
A. Yes

Q. (V) With others?
A. Yes

Q. Has anyone offered to help you resolve your problem?
A. Yes

Q. And do you want to resolve your problem?
A. I try

Q. You try. OK. In the place where you are, have you met anyone to help you resolve it?
A. No

Q. Do you want to meet someone to help you resolve it?
A. Good Bye

Apparently Sam had a lot of issues he took with him to the other side, as it were, and I ask the reader to consider how he or she might have handled Sam's sudden appearance. We were not addled in any sense, and our attitude was that we were disposed to see what help we may have been able to offer. Obviously Sam was not so disposed, and this was an opportunity to witness an entity who had departed the physical under circumstances the particulars of which we can hardly even imagine.

His decision to simply bid us good bye told us that he preferred to wallow in his resentment, and that he wasn't ready to let go. That may have been the result of excessive material attachments, or simply some emotional proclivities, or even some kind of karmic ties to his killer or killers. The important point is that we were neither judging or jumping to conclusions, but merely extending ourselves in service, and offering the highest of intentions.

We are here to learn, and in the case of the more

undesirable elements that may appear in a session, and always at the beginning, it is the emotional sobriety, speaking for myself, that dictates the tone of the exchange for us, regardless of what the entity may have in mind. Then we can inquire of our source exactly how we did in handling it.

Board Notes, 7-8-11

Q. Hello
A. Hello

Q. And who do we have with us this evening?
A. J....(long pause) KO

Q. (L) KO?
A. Yes

Q. (V) OK. We're going to stop. Do you understand that?
A. No

Q. OK. Whoever you are, you are not unwelcome here, but you have to get a hold of your energy if you want to interact with us. So please identify yourself?
A. (long pause) Fred

Q. Do we know you?
A. No

Q. OK, then please state your wishes in being here?
A. Go to hell

Q. Is that what you're saying, go to hell?
A. Yes

Q. Are you familiar with this medium?
A. No

Q. Oh, you've never been on a board before!
A. No

Q. Do you want to be an asshole, or do you want help. Use your wits and spell.
A. Fuck U

Q. Oh wow, you have an education! That was a question: do you have an education?
A. Maybe

Q. Maybe. OK. Is there something we can do for you, and if there's not, then just let us know.
A. No

Q. OK. Well then, just go your way. We wish you the best. We wish you the opportunity to find positive energies to help, because they are there. (L) They are. (V) And with that we bid you adieu. (L) Blessings. (V) Peace, and we'll ask for WF please?
A. Maybe

A. Hello.

Q. WF (his usual energetic movement in announcing himself). I know the movement (laughing)
A. Yes

Q. So I guess first of all we have to ask, what was THAT about? (L) We know, we know. We should be used to it by now. (V) But you let these people through... (L) WF's not doing it, it's us. (V) No, he lets them. He steps aside to let them through. Do you step aside to let them through?
A. Yes

Q. (L) But is it ultimately coming from us? (V) No. Is it coming from us?
A. No

Q. (V) You do that so we have an opportunity to learn!
A. Yes

Q. So in that sense, how did we handle that?
A. Well

Q. Thank you. Is there anything else you'd like to impart before we move on?
A. No.

Q. Well, I just want to say I love you for that, because that's an opportunity for growth, isn't it?
A. Yes

Q. (L) And every time something like that happens, if I didn't have a couple of beers in me I'd be running up the steps. (we both laugh). I guess to be exposed and learn how to handle it is a good thing, Yes?
A. Yes

So much for negative entities, but these were hardly the only contacts we'd had with discarnates who had made the transition to the other side. Several of Leah's departed relatives, including her father, had already contacted us, and all of them came through at the beginning of a session. The example I gave of Mozart's surprise experience was the most light-hearted, and we had such a great time with him that we were sorry to see him go, and extended him an invitation to return at any time.

The bottom line is that regardless of what one expects, or doesn't, there simply is no way to anticipate anything beyond having the highest intentions and positive energies during each and every session. If the reader has been able to appreciate the tremendous amount of information we were able to gather in the sessions as we've reported here — understanding that it only scratches the surface in the sheer volume of what we've explored, then the implications are that the only limitations of what is possible depend entirely upon your own imagination and willingness.

*   *   *

The manifestations of Spirit are infinite, and in this particular dualistic free-will universe, they can be positive or negative, with many shades of gray. The entity that you eventually decide is to be your primary contact will likely not manifest in your first session, and probably not for many sessions. It seems that the process is one of acclimation to the energies comprising the bigger picture of all the particulars involved, from the operators to the personalities that will manifest in the course of the learning experience.

One must first be able to manage the supple grasp and pressure on the planchette, or pointing device. Too much pressure and there will be no movement; too little and the fingers will slide off. Not that this is difficult to achieve, but there is also the matter of partnering with someone compatible in developing the feel for it, and being comfortable with them. One must also trust, because there is a tendency to think that the other person may be willfully manipulating the answers.

When contact is first made with any entity, a line of questions should be at the ready to try to identify who the entity is, and from where it originates. There are densities and dimensions, and while many use the terms interchangeably – not that it should matter to those for whom it really doesn't matter, it should be understood that the formerly incarnate persons who have crossed over, or died, if you prefer, are usually coming from fifth density, whereas sixth density would be more in the nature of ascended beings, and seventh the more highly angelic and archangelic. While we are in the third density physical, I cannot say that the next density, fourth, while more ethereal, would necessarily lend itself to having the facility for communicating through the board. That remains to be seen.

My suggestion would be to hold the ideal of the invocation as I've given it, or some similar spiritual attitude, and intend to make contact with a personal guide or guardian. If you believe you have actually made such a contact, use your intuition to formulate the kinds of questions regarding your personal life experiences that will elicit the kind of guidance that should be issuing from such a reliable source, and withhold judgment.

The example I've already given regarding the appearance of entities like Sam is an emotionally detached disposition that will always serve to keep you from being drawn-in to energetic tests of will, what I call emotional sobriety. Practice it at every turn where you come face-to-face with undesirables. Doing battle with any kind of discarnate will leave you drained and vulnerable, and there is nothing to be gained. This is where the attitude of service to others should be the guiding principal.

* * *

Depending on the kind of board you decide to use, there are some pointers that may help you navigate more easily through the sea of experience as it presents itself in any given session. When I first considered that I might like to explore the board's potential, I went out to the internet to see what was available, and there were plenty of choices.

Since Leah and I are artists in our own right, we decided to design and construct our own board. It was a plain blue background with black lettering, a circular alphabet, two rows of numbers horizontally inside the circle, and the Cardinal directions, one in each of the four corners of the approximately 18 inch square board. It is pictured on the front cover.

We also opted for Hello, Good Bye, Yes, No, Maybe, ?, !, and eventually added Right and Duh, as we got to know the various expressive idioms of our source. We orient 'N' to North.

I will not recommend any particular board, but I will say that I'm aware of a square spirit board that suggests mystery, is very colorful, and uses the circle format, with various zodiacal and other symbols about which I have no opinion. It also uses a circular glass disk, which is our preferred planchette, or pointing device.

We prefer the circular format because experience has shown that the circling disk going either clockwise or counterclockwise is suggestive of some aspect or other of the answer, where perhaps a counterclockwise direction offering Yes might suggest that the question, asked differently, might have a more insightful answer.

A slower circling preceding Yes often suggests there is more to the question than the simple answer would indicate. Frequently there is no movement at all, sometimes followed by a sudden move to a Yes, No or Maybe. Individual contact sources will probably develop their own idiosyncratic movements, and the operators (you) will simply have to learn them. Here are some examples of questioning sequences that demonstrate a few of these variations.

Q. So in trying to understand the mechanisms that are involved, my feeling is – and it really is a feeling, is that she has to be taking the hyaluronic acid at least twice a day. Now, will that lead to an improvement in the symptoms
A. Maybe

Q. OK. Maybe again. Are there other things that need to be added?
A. Yes

Q. And Debbie is ultimately going to be the arbiter of those things?
A. (No movement for seconds, then...) Maybe
(L) Why was that so slow?

Q. OK. Are any of the drugs or drops that she's taking now interfering with the action of the hyaluronic acid?
A. Yes

Q. Is that why you stopped right there?
A. Yes

Q. Because you knew that was going to be one of my questions!
A. Yes

I suppose it's pretty obvious what that delay was about, and this is not an unusual occurrence for us. Here is another:

Q. But avoiding the truth is how we [people] live!
A. You know it

Q. Doing, avoiding the truth is in what we do. Did you see me struggling with that issue tonight, about what you believe is what you do.?
A. Yes

Q. I was struggling that we have to get out there and represent, especially Leah and I when we're together, when we're out there. Separately or together, we have to represent. Is that engaging the truth?
A. Have more faith (I heard it before he answered)

Q. OK. Having more Faith is the doing. Is that what you're saying?
A. Yes

Leah suggesting again about representing, and I clarify that when you have faith, you ARE representing just in the fact that you have faith.

Q. When you have faith you will just be representing?
A. Yes

Q. That was a slow yes, does that mean we're getting closer to it?
A. You need to get out of it.

Q. And that means because we are not OF it!
A. Yes

In the above example, the slow Yes was a setup for a bigger statement that we probably should have arrived at on our own, because we had been told repeatedly that we are not of it, even though we are in it. And just two more, because there are many:

Q. (L) Does that mean that when, as a collective, or as part of a collective, those of us who have been working on this for years and years, when we finally click in to that mindset of transition or transformation, that they will already understand what's happening and be there already and add to the intensity?
A. Yes (large circles)

Q. That was a slow spiral to answer that because there's a little bit more involved there?
A. Yes

And the all important dramatic pause, which in this case is WF's uncanny sense of comic timing in order to make a point:

Q. But taking my place now, that isn't what Leah and I refer to as our mission, or is it?
A. ? (the disk just sat there, no movement, and then all of a sudden, whoosh! – ?)
(I laughed my ass off at that) You are so funny! (To Leah) the way he just waited, and waited, and then... (still laughing)

The point he was making was that we knew full well what it was all about, and rather than just come out and say you already know full well what it's all about, his answer was more-or-less that you should ask yourself, or, do you really need to ask, implied in the pause, followed by an unexpectedly quick zip to the ?. And this is something that will manifest when the relationship with the source is allowed to proceed as though you were talking to anyone else who happened to be in the room.

The affirmative movements are equally impressive in their opposite expressiveness, as in this example:

Q. When you say you tell us we are beautiful, and that its an energy that we have to get into understanding, and that there's some urgency, and that we might be in some imminent danger even, looking around at Japan and... So, are we in some imminent danger here?
A. No

Q. What this is really about is that the energies are culminating in some definite direction?
A. Yes (big big movements)

Q. And that was a big yes?
A. Yes

Then there are clockwise and counterclockwise circles leading to a Yes or No, or even to a sentence, and these usually connote a positive or negative situation. Here's a negative example:

I have to calm Leah down again as the disk flies out of her hand
Q. She has to calm down her energy, right?
A. Yes

Q. Part of my job is to keep her focused, right?
A. Yes

Q. A left-hand yes, right?
A. Yes.

The point in these examples is that we eventually learned to catch-on to what the slow movements, fast movements, large movements or directional circling all meant in context, and that usually involves intuiting the reason from the circumstances. This is true of every personal idiosyncrasy we have seen in the individual personalities that manifest. I would imagine this would apply equally as well if you bring a somber attitude to the board. It all translates, and you are the translator.

* * *

That brings us to the nature of the questioning itself. We have learned that it is better to begin any series of questions on any subject that can be answered with a Yes or No. In this way one can lay a foundation for questions that can be answered more thoroughly with actual statements. This rings even more true at the beginning, when one is trying to become familiar with both the process and the entities. As I said earlier, questions about one's personal experiences will be most telling in exploring the veracity of a source, and the questions are much easier to construct in a yes or no context.

And forget fortune telling: we are all altering timelines at every turn of the wheel, so what may be a seemingly certain course in one minute could likely change in the next. Probable outcomes may be a different story altogether, but it seems best to stay with information that will elicit guidance and investigative directions as opposed to having some incorporeal entity ease your mind about what is going to happen next. You will almost certainly be left at the altar if you're concerned about your partner's real intentions and want reassurance of a definite outcome.

As we began to really appreciate that we were being given an opportunity to learn faith and trust, precluding the fortune telling nature of the divining arts, we became more disposed to inquiring about the deeper nature of circumstances more as a matter of perception, allowing us to gain more navigational experience. It seems to be more valuable to learn the intuitive skills that have been conditioned out of us from birth than it is to rely on being told how something is going to play out. And where I have repeatedly demonstrated how we have had to work for answers on our own, as opposed to just being given them, we are being taught exactly that.

We had a lesson in wishful thinking versus honest investigation when Leah asked about the sale of the property we were renting. She sincerely wanted to know when the property would be sold, and had an idea when she would have liked it to be sold. We were told it would be sold in the Spring, exactly when she wanted it to be sold. I had objected to the question at the outset, but I wasn't about to become the gatekeeper at the board. It was our joint project, and we were here to learn together.

She asked the question again at another session, just checking to see that it was on track to be sold before Spring ended, and was told it would be. I was still uncomfortable with pursuing such a line of questioning, and I had done so myself. Nonetheless, I stood back and let her pursue her need to know. When it didn't happen, I knew we were going to have a lesson, whether one was intended or not. I was already working on this chapter, and had already made the statement about being left at the altar, so when the house didn't sell, I was already poised to jump on it.

Board Notes, 6-23-11

Q. You know that I have trouble with the whole fortune telling aspect of using this medium. And because anything could change at any one minute that could change anyone's fortune. (L) That's what WF says. (V) But you did indulge Leah when she was asking about the house being sold. So was your indulging her supposed to be a lesson?
A. No

Q. Because you know her expectation was the house would be sold this Spring, and we're into Summer now.
A. Wishful thinking
(L) Wishful thinking, on my part.

Q. OK. So that wasn't necessarily from you, that was her influencing the answer.
A. Maybe

Q. OK. This last chapter of the book, the instructional part, I cautioned against fortune telling. And what I said was that if you're concerned that you're going to be left at the altar, then you probably will be. So is it kind of like that warning; that's the nature of the whole thing. Like if you're asking, lotsa luck?
A. ?

Q. OK. The thing about even if you could get an answer about things like that, the timeline could change, and it could not happen anyway. Is that right?
A. It's what you make it to be.

That led in to a whole series of questions regarding focusing on what you desire, The Secret, and being able to manifest it. Leah is a natural manifester, and whatever she focuses on is almost certain to materialize. After that series we took a break, and I had to take that opportunity to mull over the fortune telling issue, and the answers we had just received about wishful thinking. When we came back from break, I went right back into it.

Board Notes, continued.

Q. Are Leah and I doing anything that we are energetically influencing the sale of this house?
A. No

Q. Can we pursue this wishful thinking statement a little more?
A. Yes

Q. So Leah was asking for information in the nature of knowing the future. Is that right?
A. Yes

Q. And then the information seemed to indicate that the house was going to sell at a certain time. Is that right?
A. Yes

Q. Now my question was, here it is, Spring's gone. The first time she asked she just said Spring. The second time she asked she said This Spring, and she was told Yes. Now you said that was wishful thinking, and I asked does that mean she was influencing the answer, and you said No. So was that... were you telling her that the house was going to be sold this Spring?
A. Yes

Q. And were you telling her that because that was what she wanted to hear?
A. Yes

Q. So the caution is be careful when you're asking something that you want to hear, because that might just be what you're told?
A. Yes
(Leah reminds us of my statement re being left at the altar)

Q. Now when I'm pursuing questions, and I don't usually ask to be told the future, but you know what I mean when I say that when I'm pursuing something you make me work for it. Is that right?
A. You need to work for it.

Q. Because that's the nature of my personality!
A. Yes

Q. And I get more benefit from that!
A. Yes

Q. So then what it comes down to is that, like in Leah's case asking when the house was going to be sold, and this would apply to anybody, when someone's on the board, it doesn't matter who the source is, and they really want a certain answer you're going to give it to them (L) or they're going to get it one way or another.
A. Yes

Q. I know we're not necessarily in the realm of reason here, but is there a reason you do something like that, like her wanting to know when the house is going to be sold. Can you tell us why you gave her the answer that she wanted to hear?
A. She needed to hear it

Q. For her peace of mind?
A. Yes

Q. And it didn't matter that she was going to come to that place where she was going to be disappointed! OK, she needed to find out that's not how it is?
A. Right

Q. And of course you know the problem I have with it is that's what she was telling [the land lady], and that (L) invalidates (V) the credibility of the source.
A. It's called free will.

Q. And you know that's a big issue for me, not necessarily in the negative sense!
A. Yes
Because you know I ask the free will question a lot: are you not telling me that because it would violate...

Q. And in [the land lady's] case the credibility thing doesn't matter because she doesn't believe it anyway?
A. Right

And she wouldn't believe it even if it happened. (L) And somewhere I accept that, what he just said.

Needless to say, lesson learned, and one that no one should have to learn themselves the hard way. I could think of hundreds of examples where such foolishness could be very very costly. I would advise more the approach that I usually take, having more of an investigative approach, verifying theories, and being willing to take a direction one may not have anticipated in order to arrive at the truth of a situation. I would also remind the reader that we were being taught and encouraged to have faith and trust, learning the higher Art of Navigation, as it were. What could be more valuable?

* * *

We have applied our board endeavors even to pursuing dream interpretation, where, for the most part, we are first required to analyze dream elements in the context of what may be going on in our lives. Then we would follow a course of Maybes or question marks, and use our intuition and intellect to sort through material that is arising from the subconscious in the dream scape. Granted that I may have been doing dream analysis for years, it is nonetheless an additional valuable tool to sort through the deeper aspects of dreaming with an objective source. For those with such interests, I would highly recommend this course.

Here are two of Leah's dreams we explored recently, that came on successive nights, but unrelated to each other. In the first she was wearing a garter, which surprised her, because she has never worn garters. It was a desert scene, and suddenly she was flying. This was also the wishful thinking session, which turned out to be a session packed with information for her.

Board Notes, 6-23-11

Q. OK. We have Leah's two dreams. The one is the garter dream, the desert, flying. Is there anything prescient in that dream?
A. It's her coming out of bondage.

Q. In her present efforts to transcend?
A. Yes

Q. So that was just like a mile post for her!
A. Yes

Q. (L) Is it prophetic?
A. Yes

Right. Because that's what the desert is. It's your bondage. The garter, (to Leah) what about the garter. (L) When I looked up the garter it was about titillation and a desire for sexual ...
Q. (V) OK. So the garter is representative of freedom, a sense of titillation, those just being symbolic of freedom!
A. Yes

Q. Is there anything else... (L) I have a question about that, and I keep thinking it's because I saw the movie Freda. That and the dream was the way I saw the scene was very much surreal like one of her paintings, and I kept wanting to paint that. Would that be an exercise that I should do? (V) OK. Would that help you in releasing that energy and acquiring that freedom, to put the symbolism into real....
A. Yes

Q. So is there anything else about that particular dream before we move on to the next one?
A. No

The significance here for Leah is that she has been developing a new persona for some years, from the time we had rekindled our relationship. I had seen her breaking loose from the old paradigm in ways that were significant for me because in my more adventurous approach to understanding the nature of reality I had long ago broken free of conventional approaches to everything.

Bondage, in my reckoning, is the programming, a theme I have repeated here at length. I was more than pleasantly surprised to hear this, and more surprised that she was given this information without our having to pry it loose, as we had in other dream explorations.

The second dream involved underground explosions, and Leah felt that she was seeing scenes that would be unfolding at some time in the future. She was right. We already analyzed that dream in the *Dreaming* chapter, but in the context of what I want to demonstrate in the value of using the board for the purpose of interpretation, I'll merely make the following two points.

This particular dream had a dual significance. First, it was in some sense prophetic, in that it appears to be an instance where a future series of events is being viewed, but we are told that we will be unaffected. Second, she was transcending the fear one would normally associate with such events, and this is a new development for her insofar as her being able to rise above something that would normally have driven her to fear.

Now I have already used examples that were much more complex, and that required a lot more work in interpreting all of the symbols involved, in the *Dreaming* chapter. Those who are pursuing such exercises in dream interpretation are encouraged to approach them as they might normally, but use the board as a feedback system, much as I have demonstrated in a multitude of issues we have pursued in many areas of our lives.

There have also been a plethora of social events and political issues we have investigated, the nature of which I hinted at in the *Inanities* chapter. But I will say that the bottom line has always been, and continues to be, the spiritual import of those issues and events.

I began this book with what may seem to have been a little heavier approach to the spiritual nature of the information that can be obtained, and certainly it reflects my own spiritual bent. I am fairly certain that this approach is rather unusual: one does not normally expect to be communing with the higher vibrational energies of one's multidimensional self. But I would suggest that there are no limits beyond one's desire for truth.

You could be a Satanist or a Shaman, but you will be connecting with sources that reflect your personal energies, and as positive or negative as those personal energies may be, you will be reflecting your own being in what manifests through those efforts. Be careful what you wish for, because you will have to live with it.

Epilogue

The entirety of the sessions included in this book occurred from mid December 2010 through the first eight months of 2011, and were all involving Leah and me, along with the occasional visitors. Leah and I had not had an easy time of our relationship, as a particular kind of issue seemed to surface almost cyclically that resulted in her completely alienating me for months. At the end of July 2011 we had our fourth major alienation, and I left.

When she visited me to return my things, she also brought the board. My feeling has always been that she had only been doing the sessions for me, so it was really no surprise. When I had conceived of taking up the board project, we were separated for our third time, and I had intended to ask my close friend and confidant Marie if she might be interested. Leah's sudden reappearance precluded that idea, and after we discussed the design, she proceeded to construct the board on her own.

None of the foregoing is to cast any aspersions on Leah, or on the quality of our relationship when we were *on*. Whatever magic comes through the accounts in this book were truly magic, for both of us, and for those who attended. Whatever issues we have to resolve, and many came up in the sessions, however they may have impacted me and/or our relationship, it takes two willing people to make it happen.

After the fifth time, we finally separated on what seems a more permanent basis, though one never knows. I wish her well, with infinite love, or it was never love at all. I know that my spiritual connection to her goes far beyond choice, but it is a conscious decision on my part to maintain a state of being that will always have her near me in one sense or another.

So when she brought me the board, I asked Marie if she'd be interested in trying it, and she jumped immediately. The first night we did a session there were logistical problems that interfered, but there was no doubt that Marie's deceased friend of several years was coming through. The next night we finally resolved all the issues that were interfering, and we had a very productive session.

It was in that session that Marie started telling me that she was picking up all the answers in her head. When we finally had a session with WF a few nights later, she insisted that she was getting the answers in her head. In fact, that session opened with her mother coming through and they were basically having a conversation between them while I did no more than contribute my hand and a few comments. She was getting every word from her mother, and then waiting for the board movements to catch up.

So the second WF session that we did, with her picking up everything, we decided at the end, with WF's concurrence, that the next session we would simply dispense with the board, and we have been doing that for about eighteen months now. Excerpts from one of the earlier sessions with Marie, from 8-31,11, is included in this book.

So will those sessions provide material for another book. I can't say just now, because much of that material is more of a personal nature, and also includes a lot of me literally duking it out with WF, a unique experience with the teacher from other lives, to say the least.

Stay tuned!

22594206R00168

Made in the USA
Lexington, KY
04 May 2013